AFTER MARS

AFTER MARS

SHANNON CASE

NEW DEGREE PRESS

AFTER MARS

ISBN: 978-1-64137-112-4   Paperback
ISBN: 978-1-64137-113-1   Ebook

For my parents.
Mom — thank you for the endless encouragement.
Dad — you're the greatest father mucker.

CONTENTS

INTRODUCTION

"Space: the final frontier.

These are the voyages of the starship Enterprise.

Its five-year mission: to explore strange new worlds, to seek out new life and new civilizations, to boldly go where no man has gone before." -Star Trek Opening, 1966

The 1960s were the height of the Space Race. Though I wasn't alive to experience it, if I had a chance to witness any time period in the world's past, this would be it. Every month seemed to bring a new "first in human history" achievement, either by the Russians or the Americans.

April 12, 1961 → First Man in Space

Russian Cosmonaut Yuri Alekseyevich Gagarin became the first human to venture into space. The Vostok 1 spacecraft made one complete orbit around Earth in 108 minutes, and reached altitudes ranging from 112 to 203 miles.

May 5, 1961 → First American in Space

United States Astronaut Alan Shepard became the first American to be launched into space. Shepard's suborbital flight lasted only 15-minutes, during which he experienced about 5 minutes of "weightlessness."

February 20, 1962 → First American in Orbit

Astronaut John H. Glenn was launched into orbit aboard an Atlas D rocket, and became the first American to orbit the Earth. Glenn made a total of 3 complete orbits, in a flight time of just 4 hours and 56 minutes.

March 18, 1965 → First Space Walk

Russian Commander Pavel I. Belyayeu and Pilot Alexei A. Leonov were launched into Earth's orbit aboard Voskhod 2. Leonov performed the first tethered space walk outside of his spacecraft while in Earth's orbit. The whole historic feat lasted just 12 minutes.

February 3, 1966 → First Spacecraft to Land on the Moon

The Russian spacecraft Luna 9 completed a 250,000-mile trip and successfully became the first spacecraft to soft-land on the Moon. Luna 9 transmitted pictures of the Moon's surface back to Earth. The mission demonstrated that the Moon's surface was strong enough to support the weight of a large spacecraft.

June 2, 1966 → First American Spacecraft on the Moon

Surveyor 1 became the first American spacecraft to soft-land on the Moon. After a journey of 63 hours and 36 minutes, Surveyor 1 successfully landed only 9 miles off its target in the Oceanus Procellarum. The spacecraft transmitted more than 11,000 high-resolution photographs before its energy sources were depleted.

September 15, 1968 → First Moon Orbit

The Soviet Zond 5 was launched. It became the first spacecraft to orbit the Moon and return.

October 11, 1968 → First Manned Apollo Mission

Apollo 7 was the first manned Apollo mission into space. The crew consisted of Walter M. Schirra, Jr.; Donn F. Eisele; and Walter

Cunningham. It made 163 orbits of the Earth in 10 days. The test flight checked life-support, propulsion, and control systems for the new Apollo spacecraft.

December 21, 1968 → First Manned Moon Orbit

Apollo 8 was launched with Frank Borman, James A. Lovell, Jr. and William A. Anders. It was the first Apollo to use the Saturn V rocket, and the first manned spacecraft to orbit the Moon, completing 10 orbits during its 6-day mission.

July 20, 1969 → First Manned Moon Landing

Apollo 11 achieved the first successful soft landing on the Moon. Neil Armstrong and Edwin "Buzz" Aldrin, Jr. became the first human beings to set foot on another world. Many experts still consider this to be the single greatest technological achievement of the 20th century.

December 15, 1970 → First Landing on Venus

The Soviet Venera 7 was the first probe to soft-land on Venus, transmitting images and data for 23 minutes. The spacecraft sent back a few images of the planet's surface before succumbing to the extreme heat and pressure of the Venusian atmosphere.

Between 1969 and 1972 there were six manned U.S. landings on the moon. As Neil Armstrong famously said on the day of the first moon walk, *That's one small step for man, one giant leap for mankind.*

But since Apollo 17 in 1972, no human has set foot on the moon, or any other celestial body, in the last 46 years. In fact, since that last mission, no human has ventured beyond low Earth orbit.

The question then becomes: *Was it truly a "giant leap"?*

"I want an Alien Bath," I proudly announced as my family ate dinner.

"A what, Honey?" my Dad asked.

"An Alien Bath," I said again, with confidence. "Aliens bathe in the snow. That's what I want."

My dad and mom were never ones to squash our dreams — particularly ones that might let them act like kids themselves — so they humored my request. Even at five years old, I knew what aliens were (turns out having a dad who is himself a nerd has its benefits).

"Okay, Honey," my dad said. "Finish your dinner and you and your sister can have an alien bath."

My sister Audrey and I giggled at the thought of an alien bath. In my head, I thought my parents would let us strip down naked and bathe in the snow piles that were forming on the deck of our suburban Connecticut home. My mom wasn't quite sure what was going to happen either, and she gave my dad a look, clearly concerned that he had just told us he was going to let us go out butt-naked in the sub-freezing temperatures.

While my mom rinsed the rest of our dishes, my dad took us upstairs to their bathroom. I whined as he carried us, clearly believing he was going back on his word of letting us dive into the snow in our birthday suits.

We kept begging for him to take us out into the snow. Instead, he kept saying, "Don't worry, you'll have an Alien Bath."

He ran the hot bath and put my sister and me into it. We continued to whine at him about breaking his promise, and when my mom came up and washed our hair, he snuck out.

SPLASH!

I whipped my head around, seeing my dad in a winter parka with a white bucket, dumping a huge pile of snow and ice into the bath. We screamed.

He picked up a second bucket, this time winding up for good effect.

SPLASH!

We screamed with joy as the icy chunks melted into our hot bath water. "ALIEN BATH! ALIEN BATH!"

My 5-year-old self continued to try to explain that this was the only rational way for aliens to bathe, because it is icy where aliens live. Of course, right?

Since that night, my sister and I would constantly beg for an "Alien Bath," in which my dad would drop snow or ice cubes into the tub with us. The simple idea of living someplace where it was completely normal to bathe in ice cubes was very exciting to me as a kid. This simple and silly family game was the start of my lifelong curiosity with living on another planet (although as an adult, Alien Baths sound much less fun).

*****

"Oddly enough, I actually think the odds [of a Mars colony] are pretty good. At this point I am certain there is a way. I'm certain success is one of the possible outcomes for establishing a self-sustaining Mars colony, in fact a growing Mars colony. I'm certain that it's possible. Whereas until maybe a few years ago I was unsure whether success was even one of the possible outcomes." -Elon Musk, CEO and founder of SpaceX, 2016

Perhaps no single man has had a greater impact on humanity's re-engagement with space exploration in the 21st century than Elon Musk.

Musk continues:

> We'll go to the moons of Jupiter, at least some of the
> outer ones for sure, and probably Titan on Saturn, and
> the asteroids. Once we have that forcing function, and
> an Earth-to-Mars economy, we'll cover the whole Solar
> System. But the key is that we have to make the Mars
> thing work. If we're going to have any chance of sending
> stuff to other star systems, we need to be laser-focused on
> becoming a multi-planet civilization. That's the next step.
>
> I'm not saying I'm skeptical of [traveling to] the stars. I
> just wonder what humanity will even look like when we
> try to do that. If we can establish a Mars colony, we can
> almost certainly colonize the whole Solar System, because
> we'll have created a strong economic forcing function for
> the improvement of space travel.
>
> It's pretty hard to get to another star system. Alpha
> Centauri is four light years away, so if you go at 10 per
> cent of the speed of light, it's going to take you 40 years,
> and that's assuming you can instantly reach that speed,
> which isn't going to be the case. You have to accelerate.
> You have to build up to 20 or 30 per cent and then slow
> down, assuming you want to stay at Alpha Centauri and
> not go zipping past.

Musk's certainty in our species' destiny as a multi-planetary one is
exhilarating — especially for a woman who grew up dreaming of
bathing in different places across the solar system. In just the past
decade of SpaceX's existence, the odds of human colonizing Mars
have gone up dramatically. Even Musk said, "When starting SpaceX
I thought the odds of success were less than 10%, and I just accepted
that I would probably just lose everything. But that maybe we would
make some progress. If we could just move the ball forward, even
if we died some other company could pick up the baton and keep
moving it forward. So that would still do some good."

Today, docu-dramas such as *Mars*, produced by Ron Howard and featuring leading space researchers and industry experts, put a colony on Mars sometime in the 2030s, just over a decade from 2018. And as much as skeptics still exist, perhaps no time since the 1960s, when space exploration was practically in our DNA – and certainly part of our collective culture – has space exploration been so possible.

In 2030, Mars. *And then. . . .*

While there is a clear path towards Mars — with SpaceX even going so far as having a motto of "Occupy Mars" — it's less clear where we'd colonize afterwards. But there are some high potential candidates:

- Will we go back to our Moon and create a colony there as both a 'staging area' for further travel AND a way to make space travel accessible to tourists on Earth?

- Could we colonize Titan, one of the moons of Jupiter?

- Would we capture an asteroid and potentially mine it for resources that are in limited supply on earth (lithium comes immediately to mind)?

- Could we travel to another star system, like Alpha Centauri, or are the challenges of the distance too great to overcome?

- Or what if we just followed the heroes in our movies and build our own "Cooper Station," like in the *Interstellar* movie?

The answer is . . . Yes.

The question, according to most experts, isn't a matter of if, but when. And with our world more curious about space exploration than at any point since the 1960s, we may be poised to build a plan for the future colonization efforts across our solar system and beyond.

This book aims to be a part of that plan. Consulting with some of the leading minds on space, colonization, human travel and science, *After Mars* is a guide for the "space nerd" in all of us who hope to make our 5-year-old dreams into a reality. *Sans* the ice baths, of course.

Admittedly, I'm not one of the world's foremost space experts, a genius in astrophysics, or frankly, even an engineer. At several points, in fact, my own fears as an "imposter" nearly held me back from writing this book. I was intimidated by the fact that I simply do not know enough. After all, how could I, an art major who barely passed first year calculus, connect myself with this world that I found so fascinating (but *so freaking math heavy*)?

I thought back to my dad and the imagination he instilled in me — a generation who grew up and now has the potential of space exploration for itself, and its children. I've been a space nerd all my life, but there was a whole world out there that I hadn't come across, simply because I wasn't looking in the right places.

"If this is important to you," my dad told me, *"no matter what, if you don't push yourself to do it, no one will do it for you. If you want to see these things happen, or make changes in the world, you need to take initiative."*

It turns out that many people share the same passion as I do for dreaming about the future of humanity. The more professors, engineers, and generally brilliant people I spoke to, the more I realized that these people whom I'd idolized throughout my childhood are people too — people who share the same love for learning and exploration. All I'd had to do was ask. Every one of the people I spoke to was genuinely invested in building a future in which humans are living off of earth, and every one of them had unique stories and perspectives to share. Just asking them to share their expertise led me to hours of interesting conversations that I could have never imagined I'd be having a year ago.

And for nearly the past year, I've talked to anyone with a shred of knowledge about space, space travel and our future:

- I've spoken to CEO's of startup companies launching innovative satellites and imaging how their technology can be used to foster space travel.
- I've interviewed researchers at MIT studying interplanetary supply chain mechanisms.
- I've talked with experts at NASA, engineers at SpaceX and designers at Mars One.
- I've contacted directors of planetariums, and professors working to engage the public with science.
- And I've even spoken to individuals slated to be among the *first* colonists of Mars (how do you get on that list!?).

The amazing part of this discussion is that I've been invited into the child-like dreams of dozens of people just like me. There's a bit of a space traveler in each of us; whether we love movies about outer space, whether we watch a solar eclipse and wonder how we fit into such a massive world, or whether we are just curious to know if we're alone.

This book is for all of us. No, we might not get to see all these things in our lifetimes, because many of them are not yet possible. But if we can help dream and support these pioneers at NASA, SpaceX and beyond, maybe one day we can truly say: *"Our five-year mission: to explore strange new worlds, to seek out new life and new civilizations, to boldly go where no man has gone before."*

Join me on the journey to discover where we'll colonize . . . after Mars.

CHAPTER 1

WHY THIS MATTERS

———

"Humanity's interest in the heavens has been universal and enduring. Humans are driven to explore the unknown, discover new worlds, push the boundaries of our scientific and technical limits, and then push further," reads the NASA exploration title page. While this is certainly true, there are numerous other practical reasons why humanity *must* leave Earth.

REASON 1: THE NEXT EVOLUTIONARY STEP

"Mankind is destined to step beyond his earthly bonds just as his ancestors once crawled out of the seas. Colonizing new worlds … the race will survive."— Charles Sheldon

Though people thought it was insane back in 1859 when Charles Darwin proposed the theory of evolution in his book, *On the Origin of Species*, it is now widely accepted. Darwin's theory of evolution posits that the process in which organisms change over time results in changes in physical or behavioral traits. Those changes allow that organism to better adapt to its environment, and therefore produce more offspring.

Humans have developed many traits and behaviors that allow us to thrive even in the harshest environments on Earth. Humans live in research facilities in Antarctica where the temperatures can reach as low as -55°C, and populate deserts where the heat reaches above 45°C in the summer. We have adapted and developed the technology to survive in the most hostile environments on Earth, but we're running out of environments to populate. This phenomenon leads some scientists to believe that our species is looking at an irreversible decline in evolutionary mutations.

Dr. Ian Tattersall, an anthropologist at the American Museum of Natural History, told National Geographic, *"Because we have evolved, it's natural to imagine we will continue to do so, but I think that's wrong."* He further explained, *"Everything we know about evolutionary change suggests that genetic innovations are only likely to become fixed in small, isolated populations."*[1]

The issue with our current state is that human populations are no longer living in small isolated populations. *"Since the advent of settled life, human populations have expanded enormously. Homo sapiens is densely packed across the Earth, and individuals are unprecedentedly mobile,"* Tattersall says. *"In this situation, the fixation of any meaningful evolutionary novelties in the human population is highly improbable."* Tattersall believes that we are at the end of human evolution, stating, *"Human beings are just going to have to learn to live with themselves as they are."*[2]

Other scientists disagree with Tattersall. They believe that humans have begun to enter an era in which we are *consciously* in control of our own evolution. No other species on earth has had this opportunity, and many have been wiped out because of it. We can choose to stay on Earth, and wither away due to our inability to

---

1 Tattersall, Ian, Dr., qtd. Owen, James "FUTURE HUMANS: Four Ways We May, Or May Not, Evolve," *National Geographic News* (https://news.nationalgeographic. com/news/2009/11/091124-origin-of-species-150-darwin-human-evolution.html), 2009.
2 Owen, 2009.

evolve, or we can choose to go to the harshest and most isolated of environments: outer space.

John Hawks, an anthropologist at the University of Wisconsin-Madison, explains. *"If we had spacefaring people who went on one-way voyages to distant stars, that might be enough to trigger speciation."* He was, however, careful to note that there are populations in remote areas on Earth that have been isolated for thousands of years and have still not developed significantly differing traits.[3]

Jelor Gallego, a journalist at Futurism.com, an online news outlet that covers breakthrough scientific discoveries and technologies, writes that, *"The minute we send independent space colonies, we are creating the perfect conditions for Darwinian evolution to continue."*[4] In order for humanity to continue to evolve, the best option is to go to space. Beyond the fact that *eventually* in order to evolve as a species we will be required to expand into space, there are important practical reasons for doing so now.

REASON 2: POPULATION GROWTH

"We are running out of space, and the only places to go to are other worlds. It is time to explore other solar systems. Spreading out may be the only thing that saves us from ourselves. I am convinced that humans need to leave Earth." -Stephen Hawking, at the Starmus festival in Norway.

An ecosystem's carrying capacity for a species may vary based on its ability to regenerate the food, water, atmosphere, and other necessities that the organisms depend on for survival. The carrying capacity for a given species is the maximum population that its ecosystem can support. Ecosystems are not able to exceed their

---

3 Ibid.
4 Gallego, Jelor, "The Next Stage of Evolution: How Will the Human Species Evolve?" https://futurism.com/the-next-stage-of-evolution-how-will-the-human-species-evolve/, 2016.

carrying capacity for long periods of time. In a situation where carrying capacity for a particular species is reached or exceeded, the food sources, water, and other necessities are depleted and the species will begin to die off. The population density for that species has become so high that the ecosystem's resources are not able to support the continued population growth. Take the story of the North American deer, for example.

Before Europeans colonized North America, deer were herbivores whose population was kept in check by wolves, a top predator of the forest ecosystem. When the European settlers came and hunted the population of wolves, it resulted in an unintended consequence: the deer population quickly began to multiply, as left unchecked by the depleted population of wolves. This led to the population of deer exceeding the carrying capacity of their environment, and as a result the deer began to starve.

The deer began to eat anything they could find, including species of plants that they hadn't before, which created a harmful ripple effect on other plant and animal life. This effect came around full circle when the deer, desperately looking for food, began to infest farms and gardens of the settlers. The settlers realized their mistake, and began to help by reducing the deer population.

In modern times there are still areas in which there is a yearly "culling" of deer, in order to reduce deer starvation and damage to crops. Other areas have tried to re-introduce the population of wolves as a means to correct the damage done, and both measures have seen positive changes in a healthier ecosystem as a result.

In the story of the North American deer, humans were the triggering factor for the deer's over population, and we're still working to correct it over 500 years later. We're on the brink of making a similar mistake again— this time with our own population. According to the United Nations, at current growth rates the human population on Earth in 2050 will reach 9.8 billion people, and will reach 11.2 billion in the year 2100.[5]

The UN data also shows that the population growth rates are falling to near "replacement level" (this means that for each woman there will be 2.1 children born), which leads many scientists to believe that the population will likely stabilize around 10 billion between the years of 2050 and 2100. While this may not seem to be a great difference in comparison to our current population of 7.4 billion, scientists like Edward O. Wilson, a sociobiologist at Harvard University, warn us that this will not be sustainable. His estimates predict that this capacity could be reached with populations as low as 10 billion people.

"The appropriation of productive land—the ecological footprint—is already too large for the planet to sustain, and it's growing larger. A recent study building on this concept estimated that the human population exceeded Earth's sustainable capacity around the year 1978. By 2000 it had overshot by 1.4 times that capacity. If 12 percent of land were now to be set aside in order to protect the natural environment, as recommended in the 1987 Brundtland Report, Earth's sustainable capacity will have been exceeded still earlier, around 1972. In short, Earth has lost its ability to regenerate—unless global consumption is reduced or global production is increased, or both." Wilson writes in his book, *The Future of Life.*

"If everyone [on the entire planet] agreed to become vegetarian, leaving little or nothing for livestock, the present 1.4 billion hectares of arable land (3.5 billion acres) would support about 10 billion people," Wilson goes on to explain. *"For every person in the world to reach present U.S. levels of consumption with existing technology would require four more planet Earths."*[6]

---

5 "Projections of Population Growth," *Wikipedia* (https://en.wikipedia.org/wiki/ Projections_of_population_growth), 2017.
6 Wilson, Edward O. *The Future of Life,* Abacus, 2002. Qtd. (http://www.elisanet.fi/ harri.nevalainen/Konsultointi/Elama/0202wilson.html).

The carrying capacity of Earth for humans is a difficult thing to determine: we constantly advance technology to keep people alive longer, invent new ways to live in previously uninhabitable environments, and develop ways to grow more food in less space. Though we may continue to push the boundaries on how many people our Earth can support, there is no doubt that one day we will reach a point at which we exceed the carrying capacity for humans on our Earth.

With this in mind, scientists are working on several proposed solutions, most of which are aimed at keeping the population below this threshold. But what if we could maintain a balance of our planet's ecosystem without limiting the growth of our population? The solution to this is to go to space. Sending colonies out into the solar system and beyond would allow the human population to grow and evolve far beyond the limited capacity available on Earth.

REASON 3: SURVIVAL OF THE SPECIES

"I believe that the long-term future of the human race must be in space," Stephen Hawking announced to the audience at Starmus, an arts and science festival in Norway. *"It will be difficult enough to avoid disaster on planet Earth in the next hundred years, let alone the next thousand, or million. The human race shouldn't have all its eggs in one basket, or on one planet. Let's hope we can avoid dropping the basket until we have spread the load."*[7]

You've probably heard stories of the asteroid that hit Earth and killed off the dinosaurs, but did you know that that was just the most recent of those five major mass extinction events that have happened in the history of earth?

---

7 "#5: Stephen Hawking's Warning: Abandon Earth—Or Face Extinction". 2017. *Big Think.* http://bigthink.com/dangerous-ideas/5-stephen-hawkings-warning-abandon-earth-or-face-extinction.

Scientists today define the major mass extinction events on Earth to be monumental losses of plant and animal species over a short period of time, or a period of history over which anywhere between 50% and 75% of life was lost. There are many questions left unanswered about the causes of these events, but evidence is being gathered every day that leads us closer to the answers.

Here's what we know so far:

Ordovician–Silurian Extinction

This was about four hundred and thirty nine million years ago, when about eighty-six percent of all life on Earth was wiped out. Scientists agree that there are most likely two possible events to have caused this: the cooling of the planet and falling sea levels. What they believe happened was *glaciation*: massive glaciers forming at the North and South Poles, sucking lots of water up from the ocean to the ice caps and eliminating the habitats of species living in the more shallow waters. The cooling of the planet was detrimental because organisms at the time were adapted to living in an intense greenhouse environment, rather than a colder environment.

This glaciation was accompanied by a fall in atmospheric carbon dioxide, which correlated with a burst of volcanic activity, which would have deposited new silicate rocks, which, in turn, would have drawn carbon dioxide out of the atmosphere as they eroded. *This* would have caused the ocean's oxygen level to deplete, leading to toxic metals on the ocean floor that would have dissolved into the water, killing organisms on the lower levels of the food chains, and starving out higher-feeding life forms in the chain.

Some scientists also believe that there was a gamma ray burst that caused the initial extinctions, because of the patterns in the way that these species died out: the ones that were deeper underwater weren't as affected. There's a hypernova in a nearby arm of the Milky Way, around 6,000 light years away from Earth from which a 10 second gamma ray burst would've burned off half the atmosphere's ozone instantly. This would have exposed all the surface organisms to a super high level of ultra-violet radiation. There's no concrete evidence that this actually happened, but it has not been ruled out.

Late Devonian Extinction

The Late Devonian extinction happened about a hundred million years later (364 million years ago), when an estimated seventy-five percent of species were lost. It is unclear whether it was a single major event or a series of events that took place over hundreds, if not thousands, of years. The trilobites, which only survived the last extinction because they had hard shells and lived deep in the ocean, nearly died *again*. Poor trilobites.

The most popular theory is the sudden growth of giant land plants (such as trees) with roots that became so deep that they released a lot more nutrients into the soil and then into the ocean. This eventually led to a skyrocketing population of algae, depleting the oxygen in the sea, which in turn killed off the animal life.

The other theory for the cause of these extinctions was an abundance of volcanic ash leading to a cooling of the planet's atmosphere. This would explain the extinctions of all the spiders and scorpion-like creatures that had been living on land.

Vertebrates did not appear on land again for another ten million years after this. So, if it wasn't for this extinction, humans probably wouldn't have evolved and there could have been some sort of spider or scorpion-like life populating earth, which would have made for a much different book here.

There was another hundred million years, nothing went wrong, things evolved, and then. . . .

Permian–Triassic extinction

. . . the Permian-Triassic extinction, happened some 250 million years ago. Also called the "Great Dying," this was the deadliest of all of the extinction events, where ninety-six percent of all species were lost.

Yes, re-read that: ninety-six percent of all species on earth were killed off.

It was the only mass extinction that included all insects, and completely killed all of the coral population. It's widely accepted that the cause was an enormous volcanic eruption, which filled the air with carbon dioxide, feeding bacteria that emitted large amounts of methane. This warmed the Earth and led the oceans to become acidic, killing off marine life.

All of life today is descended from that four percent of life that survived. From here, it's where marine life began to develop more complexity— creatures like snails, crabs, and urchins first evolved after this period.

Triassic–Jurassic extinction

And then the next extinction event happened.

This happened suddenly around two hundred million years ago. The cause? Asteroid impact. We think (two other theories involve either climate change due to volcanic eruptions or flood basalt eruptions). Before this extinction, mammals outnumbered the dinosaurs' ancestors, but after this extinction event, one of the few surviving species was the archosaurus (an ancestor of the dinosaur). Without this, the dinosaurs might never have ruled the kingdom.

This one is perplexing to scientists because it was very sudden. It's been determined that it happened in less than ten thousand years, and was the quickest of all the extinction periods, but we're still not quite sure what caused it.

"Something suddenly killed off more than 50 percent of all species on Earth, and that led to the age of dinosaurs," explains Peter Ward, a University Of Washington professor of Earth and space sciences. But that "something" – though we have theories – is still eluding us.

Cretaceous–Paleogene extinction

The most recent and well-known of the five mass extinction events is the Cretaceous-Paleogene extinction, which happened sixty five million years ago and resulted in seventy-six percent of life on Earth being lost (yes, *this* is what killed off the dinosaurs).

In the late 1970's, when geophysicists Antonio Camargo and Glen Penfield discovered the 180 km wide Chicxulub Crater off the coast of Mexico, they were looking for petroleum. While they believed that this might have been an impact crater, they were unable to prove it until years later. In 2016, a drilling project to obtain rock core samples from the impact itself confirmed then-contemporary theories.

The 10 to 15 km wide asteroid would have crashed into Earth, creating the crater and releasing about 100,000 exajoules (EJ) of energy, an amount equivalent to the energy of 10 billion atomic bombs. The unique location of the impact, in shallow water near the coast, would have released massive amounts of toxic sulfur into the air, eventually killing off all of the non-avian dinosaur species.

"All these fossils occur in a layer no more than 10cm thick," says paleontologist Ken Lacovara. *"They died suddenly and were buried quickly. It tells us this is a moment in geological time. That's days, weeks, maybe months. But this is not thousands of years; it's not hundreds of thousands of years. This is essentially an instantaneous event."*

"If humans one day become extinct from a catastrophic collision, there would be no greater tragedy in the history of life in the universe. Not because we lacked the brain power to protect ourselves but because we lacked the foresight. The dominant species that replaces us in post-apocalyptic Earth just might wonder, as they gaze upon our mounted skeletons in their natural history museums, why large headed Homo sapiens fared no better than the proverbially peabrained dinosaurs," — Neil deGrasse Tyson, *Death By Black Hole: And Other Cosmic Quandaries, 2007*

You're probably wondering why any of this is relevant. The next mass extinction event could very well include the human species, and we might even be the cause of our own demise. These five mass extinction events have occurred on Earth, and every time life has recovered. But if the goal was set to saving and preserving *life* on Earth, you'd be reading a very different book right now. People want to save *humanity*. The goal of going to space and creating colonies is more about the idea of creating our own immortality than it is about creating a better planet for all species. While I'd personally like to see us get it together and preserve most of the planet's biodiversity, that's not what this book is about.

So what could kill off *humanity*?

To sum this all up, here's a short list of the ways we might become part of another mass extinction (if we don't cause it ourselves):

Gamma Ray Burst (GRB)

What actually happens when a GRB hits earth's atmosphere? The radiation strips the atmosphere of its ozone, leaving life below exposed to the harmful ultraviolet radiation emitted by the sun. The GRB can also cause oxygen molecules to break apart closer to the surface, creating a ground-level ozone layer. While this alone wouldn't be enough to kill off humanity, it could trigger a series of events that could do so (like it is theorized to have happened during the Ordovician–Silurian extinction).[8]

Glaciation

This one is more simple: our planet could possibly experience another ice age, which would be a bummer. What most people don't realize is that Earth has been cycling through periods of glaciation for around 2.6 million years. Roughly every 100,000 years is filled with a 10,000 year period of warmth followed by 90,000 years of ice age.

"Ice ages don't just come out of nowhere - it takes thousands of years for an ice age to begin. An ice age is triggered when summer temperatures in the northern hemisphere fail to rise above freezing for years. This means that winter snowfall doesn't melt, but instead builds up, compresses and over time starts to compact, or glaciate, into ice sheets," writes Kylie Andrews, of ABC News. What would that be like?

"Assuming it was similar to the last one, then north America would be covered in ice, the whole of northern Europe, the whole of northern Asia would be covered in ice," Dr. Steven Phipps, an ice sheet and climate system modeler at University of Tasmania, told Andrews.

Though the last ice age allowed for humans to travel and populate most of the world via land bridges, should one develop now it would be devastating. An ice age would drop the sea level, closing marine channels and making coastal cities, well, just cities. And since most coastal cities thrive because of the waterways next to which they developed, remove those waterways, and you remove the backbones of those cities.

---

8 Doyle, Amanda, "How Deadly Would a Nearby Gamma Ray Burst Be?" *Astrobio Magazine* (https://www.astrobio.net/news-exclusive/deadly-nearby-gamma-ray-burst/), 2016.

In 2018, we're actually about 6,000 years overdue for an ice age, but since we've screwed up the climate so much, we've halted it from happening —for now. Dr. Phipps says, *"If you look at what was happening prior to the industrial revolution, summers were actually getting colder in the northern hemisphere. They've been getting colder for at least the last 6,000 years, so we were definitely on that trend."* Because of greenhouse gas emissions, however, that trend has been reversed. *"There's no chance of us going into an ice age now because the greenhouse gases we've put into the atmosphere during the industrial era have warmed the earth,"* Phipps warned.[9]

Volcanic Eruptions

There are two types of volcanic eruptions that pose a threat. There are sudden explosive eruptions that launch molten rock and volcanic gasses thousands of feet into the Earth's atmosphere, and there are lava eruptions which last thousands of years and spread molten material from deep below the surface of Earth.

Yellowstone National Park, in the United States, is known for being one of the most monitored super volcanoes in the world. Scientists use GPS and satellite images, along with advanced seismometers, to detect even the slightest changes in activity.

"The last eruption of Yellowstone would potentially have put ash across both American continents," says volcanologist David Pyle at the University of Oxford. *"If you take a continental land mass and you suddenly cover it with 10cm of volcanic ash, all the organic matter and trees will lose their leaves and probably die. Animals will take in chemicals which are toxic to them. The ground will suddenly be much brighter than before, so a lot of the incoming solar radiation*

---

9 Andrews, Kylie. 2018. "What Causes An Ice Age And Why Do They Matter?". *ABC News*. http://www.abc.net.au/news/science/2016-06-15/what-is-an-ice-age-explainer/7185002.

might simply be reflected back into the atmosphere, resulting in a lengthy drought."

Though a single explosive event would be devastating, most scientists believe that this alone would not be a cause to wipe out all of humanity. Explosive events have impacted humans in the past, but never wiped out our entire species.

But what about the flood lavas?

All five of the major extinctions have correlated with some sort of lava eruptions. These flood lavas last over thousands of years and are thought to be related to continental drift. They're the creators of mountain ranges and other volcanic formations. The impact of these on humanity remains unknown, as the last recorded occurrence was millions of years before humans evolved. We may not know when, where, or even exactly how to detect these eruptions, but the fact remains that they will happen eventually.

"We expect another flood lava event sometime in the next 50 million years, but I don't think anyone's got any idea where and when," Pyle told the BBC.[10]

Asteroid Impact

At dawn in early February 2013, a bolide caused by a 20m near-Earth meteoroid traveling at an estimated 42,900 miles per hour exploded in an air burst over Chelyabinsk Oblast, Russia. The explosion generated a flash of light brighter than the sun, and produced a massive shock wave, cloud of dust, and many small meteorites. Most of the energy, which was between twenty-six and thirty-three times the energy of the atomic bomb in Hiroshima, was absorbed by the earth's atmosphere.

---

10 Cox, David. 2018. "Would A Supervolcano Eruption Wipe Us Out?". *BBC*. http://www.bbc.com/future/story/20170724-would-a-supervolcano-eruption-wipe-us-out.

First eyewitness accounts of the blast were reported on Twitter, and panic spread as people were unsure of the cause of the damage. *"This explosion, my ears popped, windows were smashed... phone doesn't work,"* Evgeniya Gabun wrote on Twitter.

"My window smashed, I am all shaking! Everybody says that a plane crashed," Katya Grechannikova reported.

A person in the region would have witnessed a streak brighter than the sun flashing though the sky. A few minutes later, a loud boom, accompanied by a shock wave, would shake the city, causing glass to shatter and buildings to rumble. An hour or so later, the city would begin to smell of burning odors, such as gunpowder or sulfur.

"My heart is still beating 200 heartbeats a minute! ... I saw this terrible flash, it was red-orange! My eyes are still hurting," a witness from Chelyabinsk wrote on a local web forum. *"I turned off all the lights, sat the kids on a couch and waited... Oh, my God, I thought the war had begun."*

The resulting shock wave left around 1,500 people seriously injured, and caused damage to 7,200 buildings in six cities across the region. While most of the injuries occurred as a result of the secondary blast effects of shattered glass, direct injuries, such as flash blindness and UV burns were also reported. Thankfully, no one died during this event.

"At first I saw a huge bright fire up in the skies, and then came a loud explosion that not only shattered the windows, but blew out the window frames," Taisiya Alabuzhina told RT.[11]

---

11 "Chelyabinsk Mystery Zone: Blue Snow, Three Suns, Meteorite Explosion (VIDEOS)". 2015. *RT International.* https://www.rt.com/news/234599-meteorite-russia-chelyabinsk-mystery/.

This meteoroid was only 0.2% of the estimated size of the asteroid that hit Earth 65 million years ago and ended the age of the Dinosaurs.

Expansion of the Sun

Eventually, even if humanity survives all other devastating possibilities, our sun is slowly expanding and brightening. In approximately 7.6 billion years, our sun will expand into a red giant star and potentially swallow up the Earth in its progress. While the exact physics of how this will happen are still debated by scientists, the effect on the habitability of the planet is not.

"Life on Earth will have disappeared long before 7.6 billion years," says University of Sussex astrophysicist Dr. Robert Smith. *"Scientists have shown that the Sun's slow expansion will cause the temperature at the surface of the Earth to rise. Oceans will evaporate, and the atmosphere will become laden with water vapor, which (like carbon dioxide) is a very effective greenhouse gas. Eventually, the oceans will boil dry and the water vapor will escape into space. In a billion years from now the Earth will be a very hot, dry and uninhabitable ball."*[12]

Great. So even if humans are to survive any of the numerous possible extinction catastrophes, our Earth is eventually going to dry up into a crispy ball. If we're lucky, there's even a very high chance of being vaporized by the expanding sun. That's a pretty good reason to spread out our eggs, as Stephen Hawking would say.

These are just some of the *natural* ways that humanity could be pushed to extinction. There are numerous other ways we could cause this ourselves, including (but not limited to) nuclear war, climate change, or even a *Terminator* style robot takeover. That's

---

12 "#5: Stephen Hawking's Warning: Abandon Earth—Or Face Extinction". 2017. *Big Think*. http://bigthink.com/dangerous-ideas/5-stephen-hawkings-warning-abandon-earth-or-face-extinction.

some heavy stuff, but don't lose hope— we don't have to stay on this planet. *"I really think there are two fundamental paths: One path is we stay on Earth forever, and some eventual extinction event wipes us out. I don't have a doomsday prophecy, but history suggests some doomsday event will happen. The alternative is, become a spacefaring and multi-planetary species... Either we spread Earth to other planets, or we risk going extinct. An extinction event is inevitable and we're increasingly doing ourselves in"* - Elon Musk at the Wall Street Journal's D11: All Things Digital Conference in 2013

In order for our species to survive our eventual planetary destruction, we need to colonize other planets. It is inevitable that eventually the conditions to harbor human life on Earth will no longer exist. Whether you believe that it will be in the far distant future or that it could happen tomorrow, there is no avoiding the fact that life on our planet has an expiration date. But humanity does not have to. We have the ability to develop technology that will allow us to leave this planet and survive on another.

"If humanity is to continue another million years, our future lies in boldly going where no one else has gone before." - Stephen Hawking

I have no doubt that we are going to leave the planet eventually. The question remains, why not now?

REASON 4: INNOVATION

"Whatever the needs or urges — be they geopolitical, military, economic — space becomes that frontier. Not only do you innovate, these innovations make headlines. Those headlines work their way down the educational pipeline. Everybody in school knows about it. You don't have to set up a program to convince people that being an engineer is cool. They'll know it just by the cultural presence of those activities. You do that, and it'll jump-start our dreams." - Neil DeGrasse Tyson, 2012

Making the case to go to space, economically speaking, will always be difficult. There's no real business model for colonization, and the shipment of resources from other planets back to ours is too expensive to be successful. So why spend billions of dollars to go?

Exploring space has ALWAYS led to innovations here on Earth. Technologies invented for the purpose of traveling to other planets will continue to be modified and used for purposes other than originally intended. Everything from CAT Scans to Laptop Computers and Nike Trainers came from technology that was researched and developed for use in space. One simple example of this is the Dustbuster.

When NASA sent astronauts on the Apollo missions to the moon, one of the most important tasks was the collection of rock and soil samples to bring back to Earth. Most of this material was to be gathered on the surface, but in order to do a full analysis of the moon's crust, scientists on Earth would need samples of the subsurface soil. This sparked the need to develop a special drill capable of extracting core samples from as deep as 10 feet below the lunar surface. The drill would need to be powerful and capable of cutting through the hard lunar surface layer, yet be lightweight, compact and efficient. In addition, it would need to have its own power source, as the drill would be taken to locations far away from the power sources at the Lunar Module.

When NASA tasked Black & Decker to create the drill, they specially developed a computer program in order to optimize the design of the drill's motor in order to ensure that it would consume minimal power. They developed a drill with a battery-powered magnet-motor system, a system that was eventually used to collect samples on the Apollo missions.

While NASA scientists worked to analyze the lunar samples, Black & Decker engineers worked to design cordless power tools for consumer use. The company used the same computer program to design a line of power tools called the Mod 4 series, which included a shrub trimmer, lantern, grass shear, drill and a Spot Vac. They were all powered by a single interchangeable and rechargeable battery pack.

In 1974, just five years after Neil Armstrong and Buzz Aldrin became the first men to set foot on the moon, Black & Decker released the Mod 4 series. The series was a marketplace flop. However, when researching the series, it was noticed that the Spot Vac (patented by Mark Proett) had been the most successful of the tools. Studies showed that the tool had been borrowed from the workbench and used by women to clean up small spills in the kitchen and home.

This inspired Carroll Grantz, who was the manager of the Black & Decker United States Consumer Power Tool Division's Industrial Design Department at the time. He took on the task to completely re-design the Spot Vac, taking it from a power tool to a home appliance, earning Black & Decker its first-ever design patent. In January of 1979, the Spot Vac was launched with a new look, as well as a new name: the "Dustbuster." Black & Decker sold over a million Dustbusters in just that first year, and in 1995, the Smithsonian placed an original 1979 Dustbuster on display in their electrical collection at the National Museum of American History.

The product has since been redesigned several times, but is still on the market today. It is estimated that over 100 million Dustbusters have been sold since the last moon landing.[13]

Here's just a short list of things we wouldn't have without Space Exploration:

- camera phones

---

13 "NASA Spinoff Database". 2018. *Spinoff.Nasa.Gov*. Accessed May 11. https://spinoff.nasa.gov/database/spinoffDetail.php?this=/spinoff//jsc/JSC-SO-105.

- scratch resistant lenses
- CAT scans
- LED's
- Land mine removal
- athletic shoes
- foil blankets
- water purification systems
- Dustbusters
- ear thermometers
- home insulation
- the jaws of life (tool to help people in car wrecks)
- wireless headsets
- memory foam
- freeze dried food
- adjustable smoke detectors
- baby formula
- artificial limbs
- the computer mouse
- portable computers

While the Dustbuster is a fun, simple spinoff from the Apollo missions, innovations for colonizing other planets could be essential to protecting life on earth as well.

For example, scientists working to develop ways to modify and grow food on a moon such as Titan, could use the spinoff technology to create new ways to farm here on Earth. Research into the effects and treatment of radiation exposure could lead to scientists finding a cure for cancer.

"The intangible desire to explore and challenge the boundaries of what we know and where we have been has provided benefits to our society for centuries." - NASA exploration page

REASON 5: EXCITEMENT

"It's important to have a future that is inspiring and appealing. I just think that have to be reasons that you get up in the morning and you want to live. Why do you want to live? What's the point? What inspires you? What do you love about the future? And if the future's not including being out there among the stars and being a multi-planet species, it's incredibly depressing if that's not the future we're going to have." - Elon Musk

The idea of living in a spacefaring society has captivated audiences long before the technology to get there was possible. In 1902, the French film, *Le Voyage dans la Lune (A Trip to the Moon),* based on the works of Jules Verne and directed by Georges Méliès, was released. The short film, which depicts an expedition to the Moon by a group of astronomers, became an international sensation. The film was pirated and spread across the globe (though Méliès rarely received credit) and was particularly popular in the United States. The twelve-minute, hand-colored film is one of the first in the genre of human space travel, and it's theatrical nature had impact on the genres of science fiction, musicals, and avant-garde films.

There is a reason that people love films and media that choose space as a setting— because a world in which humans are multi-planetary (be it to visit or to stay) is fundamentally more exciting than a world in which we are not. We can love science fiction, even when movies like *Star Wars* consistently contradict the laws of physics, because the stories are too great *not* to love. But what about what's *actually* possible?

Last fall, I was working late in the painting studio, trying to figure out how to paint in perspective without atmospheric distortion. We had just had a lecture on painting techniques, and one of the topics was how to paint in atmospheric perspective. In order to render scenes realistically, a painter will blur out the objects that are smaller and further back, because earth's atmosphere causes a small amount of distortion when we look through it towards objects in the distance. When our professor brought this up, what immediately came to my mind was a story that someone had once told me about the missions to the moon. A friend who worked at NASA had told me that when the first astronauts set foot on the moon, they were perplexed by the difference between the visual distance and actual distance between objects. Because their eyes were used to the atmospheric distortion on Earth, they would judge objects that were in clear focus to be smaller and closer than they actually were.

I was working on a painting of a version of the Curiosity Rover situated in a landscape distinctly lacking atmospheric perspective, when I saw a post notification from Elon Musk's Instagram light up across my phone. I put down my wet brushes and opened the video. Part one featured a gorgeous animation of a group of people boarding a boat, and then crossing a bridge into a massive rocket. The rocket launched and the video paused. "NOOOOO!!!!" I hastily clicked on part two, and my eyes welled up with tears at the rendering of a rocket speeding across the earth, taking these people from NYC to Shanghai in less than 40 minutes, while text scrolled faster and faster, eventually proclaiming the BFR could take humans anywhere on Earth in under an hour.

I put my phone down as tears streamed down my face. I couldn't help but be overwhelmed with excitement. I've obviously seen things on TV and in science fiction, but I'd never seen a visual that had moved me so much. The power of that animation was its ability to convince me of the fact that these things were truly possible. Watching these renderings from the man who pledges to actually build them, and who plans to get manned missions to Mars in just 8 years, blew me away. I sat in the studio, looking at the painting I had been working on, and let myself go. My mind raced from thoughts on the human scale of this technology to what it means in the context of an interplanetary species.

On the human scale, this would mean that someone could visit family across the globe in a fraction of the travel time. Immediately I thought of my grandmother, whose bad back has limited her ability to travel internationally for years. When this technology becomes a reality, she'll be able to get in a rocket and arrive at my cousin's home in Ireland in less than the time that it takes for her to drive from her house to the nearest airport now.

"Becoming a multi-planet species, beats the hell out of being a single-planet species" - Elon Musk, talking about going to Mars.

Over the course of writing this book, I've interviewed experts in all different areas related to space. When I asked them what the most inspiring thing they'd ever seen related to space was, by far the most common answer was, "A rocket launch." Nothing is truly awesome, in the real sense of the word, short of seeing a million-pound rocket blast off before one's very eyes. The immensity of space, and the ability of humans to work together to create technology capable of exploring it, will never get old.

"Spreading out into space will completely change the future of humanity. I hope it would unite competitive nations in a single goal, to face the common challenge for us all." - Stephen Hawking

Beyond enabling individuals, access to space spinoff tech like the BFR in terrestrial travel will shrink the borders around the world, and create broad new opportunities for international relationships. When the world feels as though it is shrinking, people will feel pushed to expand. Where can we go next? Mars is the obvious answer, but where after that?

"Man must at all costs overcome the Earth's gravity and have, in reserve, the space at least of the Solar System. All kinds of danger wait for him on the Earth . . . We have said a great deal about the advantages of migration into space, but not all can be said or even imagined." — Konstantin Tsiolkovsky, The Aims of Astronautics, *1929*

CHAPTER 2

BIG F*CKING ROCKETS

The first step to getting off Earth— you guessed it: literally getting cargo (including fragile humans) off the planet. When we talk about space colonization, the first questions that might pop up are "How will we survive there?" or "What will we do there?", but what we should be asking is, "How will we get there?"

In the movies, we see our heroes traveling faster than the speed of light, arriving nearly instantaneously at each destination. But this isn't the movies, and "science-fiction easy" isn't always "real-world easy." So what are the possibilities? How far are we from being able to travel, not just to Mars, but beyond? And, what, exactly, is a rocket?

The word rocket is typically used describe a type of engine, but can also be used to talk about the vehicle that is carried by a rocket engine. Rocket engines burn fuel in order to produce thrust. The fuel burned in rockets is pushed out as hot gas, lifting the rocket away from the earth. Unlike a jet engine, which relies on oxygen in the air to work, rockets must carry all the fuel they need to space.

There are two main types of rocket engines: some use liquid fuel, and others use solid fuel. Rockets, like those on the Space Shuttle orbiter, use liquid fuel, while the boosters use solid fuel. Solid fuel rockets have been around since fireworks were first used in China in the 1200's. Liquid fuel rockets, in comparison, are relatively new — American scientist Robert Goddard flew the first one in 1926.[1]

While early rockets used to send U.S. Astronauts to space were developed by the military, eventually NASA began developing its own rockets. The first of these was the Saturn family.

Saturn V was the rocket used to send Neil Armstrong, and every man following him, to the moon. To this day, Saturn V has remained the tallest, heaviest, and most powerful rocket ever launched from Earth. It is the only rocket to have ever taken humans beyond low Earth orbit.

There were a total of 15 flight-capable vehicles built, and 13 were flown. The two remaining rockets were designated for the cancelled Apollo 19 and 20 missions, and now have parts displayed in museums and space centers across the country. Each Saturn V launch cost somewhere around $185 million (that's 1.2 billion dollars *per rocket* in today's dollars), and were fully expendable.

With the end of the Apollo missions, NASA and the rest of the space agency set its sights closer to home: low Earth orbit. The final Saturn V rocket was used in 1973 to launch the Skylab, the United States' first space station, and a predecessor to the ISS. The Space Shuttle program, officially known as the *Space Transportation System,* was developed. The Space Shuttle consisted of an orbiter, which launched with two reusable solid rocket boosters and a disposable fuel tank. The orbiter of the Space Shuttle was a reusable space plane that could deliver humans and cargo to low earth orbit, as well as return and land like a traditional aircraft.[2]

---

1 Wild, Flint. 2018. "What Is A Rocket?". *NASA*. https://www.nasa.gov/audience/forstudents/5-8/features/nasa-knows/what-is-a-rocket-58.html.

2 "The Space Shuttle Decision". 2018. *History.Nasa.Gov*. https://history.nasa.gov/SP-4221/ch6.htm.

The last Space Shuttle launch was in 2011, and since then, NASA has sent all of its astronauts to the ISS aboard Russian Soyuz rockets (ironic, I know). Yep— since that last launch in 2011, NASA has not produced a rocket capable of sending humans to space, even just to the ISS in LEO. So . . . what happened?

It wasn't for lack of technological know-how; it was politics and policy changes that really threw NASA behind in the rocket game. Because NASA is a government agency, it is subject to control from the Executive Branch, and with each president elected, the goals and programs can change dramatically.

"So what's happened throughout all of space history after the Apollo program was over was to start, stop, start, stop, cancel." explains Dr. Peter Diamandis, founder of X PRIZE. As Diamandis says, one president says we're going to the Moon, the next sets the sail for Mars, and the next comes and says we're headed back to the Moon, leading to a point where *"the agency is unable to sustain consistent funding to do anything."* Diamandis continues, *"The scientists and engineers at NASA are amazing and they've done extraordinary things. But they're risk aversion. That doesn't allow us to do new and novel things that are on the edge. Doing anything big and bold in space is hard and it's risky. So, it's entrepreneurs taking the risks these days, willing to put everything on the line."*[3]

While there currently isn't a NASA rocket able to take humans anywhere, there are plans to create a new class of launch vehicles that are able to take humans to low Earth orbit and beyond.

---

3 Lee, Nathaniel, David Anderson, and Jessica Orwig. 2018. "The Surprising Reason Why NASA Hasn't Sent Humans To Mars Yet". *Business Insider*. http:// uk.businessinsider.com/why-nasa-has-not-sent-humans-to-mars-2018-2?r=US&IR=T.

SPACE LAUNCH SYSTEM (SLS) AND ORION

NASA is currently working on the largest rocket ever built for human exploration missions beyond Earth's Orbit. The goal is to be flexible, they want to be able to use it to go to low Earth orbit and deliver crew and supplies to the ISS, but also send large payloads beyond LEO, further into the solar system. The goal of the early missions is to develop a launch system with the capability of sending humans, habitats, and support systems into deep space. The first Orion Spacecraft missions aim to establish procedures and answer questions that will open the possibilities for deep space exploration in the future.

While the initial missions for SLS are not planned for Mars (this is fickle and really depends on who's in power when it becomes ready), this is the type of vehicle that humans will need to make the trip to Mars or any other planet.

TECH & SPECS FOR THE SLS:

"SLS, the world's most powerful rocket, will launch astronauts in the agency's Orion spacecraft on missions to an asteroid and eventually to Mars, while opening new possibilities for other payloads including robotic scientific missions to places like Mars, Saturn and Jupiter."
—NASA, Exploration Systems Development, 2017

Engines

The SLS features four RS-25 engines, which are upgraded engines from the space shuttle inventory. One RS-25 could power 846,591 miles of residential street lights (that's long enough to go to the moon and back, and then circle the Earth 15 times). Aerojet Rocketdyne is the main contractor.

Boosters

The SLS will use two, 5-segment solid rocket boosters. If the heat produced by these boosters could be converted to electric power, firing them for two minutes would supply enough kilowatt hours of power to support 92,000 homes for a full day. Orbital ATK is the prime contractor working on these.

Core Stage

This section of the rocket includes the avionics that control the vehicle during flight, and also holds 730,000 gallons of supercooled liquid hydrogen (-253°C) and liquid oxygen (-183°C) to fuel the RS-25's. The Boeing company is working with NASA to build this 200-foot tall, 27.6-foot diameter part of the rocket.

Obviously, these are not yet completed, and we are not sending people to Mars tomorrow. However, the developments of each of these components has progressed enough that there are both crew and cargo configurations planned for the SLS. Travel to Mars may not be eminent, but it is close.

Block 1: Human spaceflight

The Orion Crew Vehicle will sit atop this version of the SLS, standing taller than the Statue of Liberty, at 322 feet tall. When fueled, the rocket will weigh 5.75 *million* pounds, and will carry more than three times the mass of the space shuttle. The Block 1 configuration of the SLS will produce the equivalent thrust of more than 160,000 Corvette engines, totaling 8.8 million pounds of force at liftoff. This is 15% more than the thrust of the last Saturn V liftoff in 1973.

This is the first configuration planned for the SLS, and will be used in the Exploration Mission-1.

Block 2: Cargo

For future missions, NASA needs to create a rocket with even more power. The Block 2 is an evolved configuration of the SLS, featuring a more powerful second stage and boosters. It will weigh 6.5 million pounds and provide 9.2 million pounds of thrust at liftoff. The idea behind the block 2 cargo configuration is to create a workhorse vehicle capable of accomplishing a human mission to Mars, and beyond.

TECH & SPECS FOR ORION:

"Drawing from more than 50 years of spaceflight research and development, the Orion spacecraft is designed to meet the evolving needs of our nation's deep space exploration program for decades to come"—NASA, Exploration Systems Development, 2017

Orion is the exploration vehicle that will carry four crew members to space, sustain astronauts during their missions, provide emergency capabilities, and ensure safe re-entry from deep space return velocities. Orion's missions are designed to pave the way for human spaceflight beyond low Earth orbit, and are slated to begin in the early 2020's. Though the timeline has been continually pushed back, the technology being developed will ensure the safety of the crew. Such technology includes a revolutionary new launch abort system, life support, propulsion, thermal protection, redesigned avionics systems, and other elements developed to facilitate the integration of new innovations in order to enable extended duration of deep space missions.

There are three primary parts of the Orion spacecraft: the Launch Abort System, the Crew Module, and the Service Module.

Launch Abort System

This is the part of the vehicle that is designed to protect the astronauts in the event of an emergency. The Launch Abort System is positioned above the crew module at the top of the spacecraft. Designed to protect the astronauts from a failing rocket, the system can activate within milliseconds, pulling the crew to safety and positioning the module for a safe landing. The Launch Abort System's abort motor generates enough thrust to lift 26 elephants off the ground, and produces the same power as five and a half F-22 Raptors combined.

Crew Module

The crew module is capable of transporting four crew members beyond low-Earth orbit, providing a safe habitat from launch, all the way through landing and recovery. Designed to dock in space with a larger habitat module, the Orion crew module is equipped to allow a crew to remain in space for a lengthier time than has previously been possible.

Orion engineer Stuart McClung goes so far as to say that he considers the 16ft spacecraft spacious when compared to the Soyuz capsule, currently used to send astronauts to the International Space Station. While giving a tour of working models for the spacecraft, McClung pointed to the Orion crew module and explained, "*This is like a big stretch limo compared to that Soyuz capsule.*"

Service Module

The service module of the Orion spacecraft is being designed by the European Space Agency. It will provide support for the crew module, in-space propulsion capability, attitude control, and high-altitude ascent aborts. It also provides oxygen, nitrogen, and water to the crew module living environment, and can also hold unpressurized cargo. The service module generates and stores power while in space, and provides the primary thermal control for the spacecraft.

The politics of NASA missions are constantly changing, and the specifications of a Mars mission using SLS and Orion have not been set. Of course, this begs the question: If we're not taking the most powerful rocket ever built straight to Mars, where are we going first?

FIRST MISSION: EXPLORATION MISSION-1 (EM-1)

"NASA and its partners will use this proving ground to practice deep-space operations with decreasing reliance on the Earth and gaining the experience and systems necessary to make the journey to Mars a reality."—NASA, *The Ins and Outs of NASA's First Launch of SLS and Orion*

Orion's first mission, Exploration Mission-1, will be an unmanned journey that will send the spacecraft on a three-week mission, traveling thousands of miles beyond the moon. This will be the farthest distance that a spacecraft designed specifically for humans will have ever gone. While the launch date has been pushed back multiple times, acting NASA Administrator, Robert Lightfoot, has committed to keeping the goal of a late 2019 launch. *"While the review of the possible manufacturing and production schedule risks indicate a launch date of June 2020, the agency is managing to December 2019,"* Lightfoot says. Though the exact date may change due to manufacturing and production delays, the launch of EM-1 will mark an exciting beginning to America's next era of space exploration.

"Hardware progress continues every day for the early flights of SLS and Orion. EM-1 will mark a significant achievement for NASA, and our nation's future of human deep space exploration," said William Gerstenmaier, associate administrator for NASA's Human Exploration and Operations Mission Directorate in Washington.

"Our investments in SLS and Orion will take us to the Moon and beyond, advancing American leadership in space."

According to NASA, the mission will blast off from Launch Complex 39B at NASA's Kennedy Space Center in Florida. After initial blast off, the spacecraft will deploy its solar arrays and the SLS upper stage, known as the Interim Cryogenic Propulsion Stage (ICPS). This is what will give Orion the push needed to leave Earth's orbit on its course towards the moon. Once ready, the Orion will separate from the ICPS and continue on its course, propelled by the service module. The ICPS will complete its own mission in which it will deploy small satellites, called CubeSats, which will perform experiments and technology demonstrations. Orion will then fly through the Van Allen radiation belts, pass the GPS satellite constellation, and make the switch from communicating via NASA's Tracking and Data Relay System satellites to communicating through the Deep Space Network.

The next leg of the journey will take several days, requiring constant monitoring from engineers who will supervise the craft's systems, as well as ensure Orion's trajectory. Once Orion reaches the moon, it will fly 62 miles above the surface and use the gravitational force to propel itself into a retrograde orbit approximately 40,000 miles from the moon. Orion will orbit the moon for six days, collecting data and providing time for mission controllers to assess its performance.

Orion will then begin its return journey to Earth, starting with another flyby. This time, the spacecraft will fly within 60 miles of the moon's surface and time a precise firing of the service module to propel itself back towards Earth's atmosphere, which it will enter at a speed of 25,000 miles per hour. This will cause the spacecraft to heat to a temperature of nearly 2,800 degrees Celsius before it splashes down in the Pacific Ocean, off the coast of San Diego, California.

"This is a mission that truly will do what hasn't been done and learn what isn't known," said Mike Sarafin, EM-1 mission manager at NASA Headquarters in Washington. *"It will blaze a trail that people will follow on the next Orion flight, pushing the edges of the envelope to prepare for that mission."* Preparations are already being made for the next two crewed Orion missions.

Government programs that are developing rockets that can go further and carry more than ever before have led to innovations in manufacturing that affect not only the aerospace industry, but other manufacturing and high-tech industries as well. More than 100 parts of Orion will be manufactured using 3-D printing, and while welding parts of the core stage, NASA used self-reacting friction stir-welding to weld the thickest structures ever joined. As cool as this is on its own, however, there is an added bonus to having this type of development: it strengthens the economy. Technology R&D contributes to the growth of a nation's economy in ways that many other areas seldom contribute.

"Economists have long known that technological advance is the primary source of higher productivity and economic growth, and that research and development (R&D) is the chief contributor of technology. What is new is the preponderance of recent evidence that high-technology efforts such as the Shuttle and other space programs have a more potent effect on the economy than most other forms of R&D activity." - NASA history archive [4]

While companies like Aerojet Rocketdyne and Orbital ATK are contracted to make parts of NASA's rockets, there are companies dedicated to reinventing the way rockets are manufactured. One of those companies was founded by a man whose name has become synonymous with innovation: Elon Musk.

---

4 "Economic Impact Of Space Shuttle". 2018. *History.Nasa.Gov.* https://history.nasa.gov/SP-407/part4.htm.

As legend tells it, Elon Musk read the book *Hitchhiker's Guide to the Galaxy*, which begins with the premise that Earth has been destroyed to make way for an intergalactic bypass, and was inspired to start a company that would prevent the loss of humanity should something like this actually occur. When it comes to the aerospace industry, it's difficult to comprehend just how much money is spent on building and launching things into space, and.Musk's initial entry into the industry was met with skepticism. Few people believed that launching rockets was a task impossible for one small start-up to accomplish.

"When Elon Musk said he was going to launch his rocket and then land the first stage on a barge, I thought he was crazy," NASA Astronaut Scott Kelly admits. *"And then he did it. I'm not going to ever doubt what he says, ever again."*[5]

Today, SpaceX is a company that pays its bills by launching rockets with payloads for the U.S government and other private satellite companies. The profits from these missions are what let. SpaceX fund its real mission: getting a colony to Mars.

What's the number one thing stopping humanity from going to Mars? The cost to get there. Musk founded SpaceX in order to compete with the larger, bureaucratic companies who dominate the industry. What also sets SpaceX apart is that, unlike its competitors, the Hawthorne, CA based company designs and manufactures almost every part of its rockets itself.

SPACEX (SPACE EXPLORATION TECHNOLOGIES): FALCON HEAVY AND DRAGON CAPSULE

Though through the use of Falcon Heavy, SpaceX aims to make the cost per pound closer to $1,000 per pound, *"Clearly that's still*

---

5 Sheetz, Michael. 2018. "Don't Doubt Elon Musk, Says Astronaut Who Spent A Year In Space". *CNBC.* https://www.cnbc.com/2017/10/17/astronaut-scott-kelly-says-dont-doubt-elon-musk.html.

too much," Musk says. *"We really need to get to well under $100 a pound."*[6] So What is SpaceX doing to smoke the competition?

The company began by developing a rocket whose booster could land vertically on land or at sea, and be fully recovered and reused. Reusing rockets is important because it allows for the company to launch more often and without having to re-manufacture each launch. This makes building each rocket far more cost-effective.

SpaceX's main rocket is the Falcon 9, which is a two-stage launch vehicle powered by 9 Merlin rocket engines. And while they may have made history when they landed the first stage, and again when they successfully launched a refurbished rocket, and while the Falcon 9 is great for taking cargo to and from the ISS, in order to get to Mars, there needs to be a bigger option.

You've probably heard of Elon Musk launching his car into orbit. The reason? When testing rockets, usually a mass simulator (read: bunch of bricks/heavy things), is used for the maiden payload in order to test the weight capacity with something inexpensive— just in case something goes wrong and it blows up. Musk, who has a flare for creating a spectacle, wanted to spice his launch up and send something a little more exciting.

In February 2018, SpaceX launched the Falcon Heavy rocket for the first time. Standing at a height of 70m (229.6 ft), with the capacity to launch 57 metric tons of cargo into space, SpaceX's Falcon Heavy became the most powerful operational rocket in the world — twice as powerful as any other rocket in existence. Its maiden voyage on February 6th, 2018 marked the beginning of an exciting new era for the space industry.

---

6 "Spaceflight Is Getting Cheaper, But Not Enough". 2018. *NPR.Org*. https://www.npr.org/sections/money/2011/07/21/138166072/spaceflight-is-getting-cheaper-but-its-still-not-cheap-enough.

The Falcon Heavy consists of essentially three of Falcon 9's nine-engine cores strapped together, for a total of 27 Merlin engines. SpaceX claims that the rocket could lift the equivalent of a fully loaded 737 jetliner into orbit (that's including passengers, luggage, and fuel).[7]

"Watching the Falcon Heavy rise above the historic pad that has been the launch point for so many critical missions is a true testament to the hard work transitioning our nation's launch infrastructure in support of the commercial launch industry." Robert Lightfoot, NASA Administrator, announced after the historic launch.[8]

SpaceX also designs its own spacecraft capable of carrying cargo, and hopefully humans, to orbit as well.

Dragon Capsule:

"It is the only spacecraft currently flying that is capable of returning significant amounts of cargo to Earth. Currently Dragon carries cargo to space, but it was designed from the beginning to carry humans."—SpaceX Website

In 2006, SpaceX began development of Dragon (along with Falcon 9) under a $278 million Commercial Orbital Transportation Services (COTS) contract with NASA. These COTS contracts were part of a program trying to create innovation in the commercial arena, as NASA was winding down the space shuttle program. It was designed to bring cargo (and eventually crew) into LEO and the ISS, and, hopefully, beyond.

"The air mail program was a huge boost when the Post Office went commercial, and that resulted in explosion of innovation and improvement in technology. It really was the dawn of aviation in America where it went from joy rides that rich people could do,

---

7 "Falcon Heavy". 2018. *Spacex*. http://www.spacex.com/falcon-heavy.
8 Granath, Bob. 2018. "Falcon Heavy: A Multi-User Spaceport Success Story". *NASA*. https://www.nasa.gov/feature/falcon-heavy-a-multi-user-spaceport-success-story.

to today where aviation is accessible to almost everyone. I think historically COTS program will be seen in that light." - Elon Musk

Though delayed multiple times, often due to explosions, SpaceX worked tirelessly to develop both the Falcon 9 rocket and the Dragon, all on a budget that was a small fraction of the size of other aerospace companies. In June 2010, SpaceX celebrated the first successful launch of its Falcon 9 rocket, topped with a stripped down version of the Dragon Capsule. By December of the same year, the first version of Dragon was ready to make its maiden flight.

On the morning of December 8, 2010, hundreds of SpaceX employees excitedly waited as SpaceX prepared to launch its first test flight of the Dragon Capsule from Launch Complex 40 at Cape Canaveral Air Force Station. The first launch window, beginning at 14:03 UTC (just after 6 am for those watching from SpaceX headquarters in Hawthorne, California), was aborted due to a small fault in data. The next window, just over an hour and a half later allowed SpaceX to successfully launch COTS Demo Flight-1.

The mission lasted a total of just 3 hours, 19 minutes, and 52 seconds from launch to landing, but was successful in launching a small payload of satellites into Low-Earth Orbit, while the Dragon circled the Earth twice, and then returned to land in the Pacific Ocean 800km off the coast of Mexico, splashing down within 10km of its target.

In the days following the launch, SpaceX revealed that Dragon was indeed carrying a secret payload: **a wheel of cheese**. SpaceX CEO Elon Musk revealed to reporters that the wheel of Le Brouere cheese was sent up to honor a skit from the British comedy show Monty Python's Flying Circus. *"If you like Monty Python, you'll love the secret,"* Musk told reporters after the launch.

SpaceX packaged the cheese in a top secret compartment securely bolted within the Dragon Capsule. SpaceX officials stated, *"It was a payload so secret, SpaceXers made it 'Top Secret' (think Val Kilmer 1984, not official US Government),"* in a reference to the comedy film *Top Secret!*

From that first flight in 2010, Dragon has been making history with each iteration of the program:

- The 2010 launch marked the first time a commercial spacecraft had ever successfully been recovered from orbit.

- The 2012 lunch of the Dragon Capsule made history when it became the first non-government (private commercial) spacecraft to deliver cargo to the International Space Station and return cargo back to Earth.

- Since then, SpaceX has now completed 14 resupply missions to the ISS using the Falcon 9 and Dragon.

But, like I said, resupplying the ISS is just a way to pay the bills for SpaceX— a company whose mission is to create a self-sustaining human habitat on Mars. The next steps for Dragon will involve launching people in the crew cabin, and, eventually, pairing it with the Falcon Heavy in order to enable missions deeper into space.

"People sometimes think the difference between cargo and crew required enormous amount of magical pixie dust. This is not the case. If there would have been people sitting in Dragon today, they would have had a nice ride, feeling about 4-5 G's, which is about what an amusement park ride is like."—Elon Musk, after the first successful launch of the Dragon capsule in 2010

Cargo Dragon:

Dragon is split between two sections: a pressurized section designed to carry both humans and cargo, and a trunk, which supports the upper section during the ascent to space. The pressurized section of Dragon contains the draco thrusters (used for maneuvering and attitude control), the guidance and navigation control, and a heat shield. The trunk carries unpressurized cargo and houses the solar arrays. Altogether, the Cargo Dragon can hold 25 cubic meters (883 cubic feet) of total cargo volume.

Crew Dragon (Dragon 2):

The crew version of the dragon features an environmental control and life support system, and a launch abort system that is integrated directly into the spacecraft. This means that Crew Dragon is protected from launch up until it reaches orbit, using eight SuperDraco rocket engines built into the walls and capable of moving the spacecraft over half a kilometer in just over 5 seconds.

This is a vehicle designed, from its conception, to bring humans to the red planet and, eventually, beyond. For now, though, we'll have to be content with the fact that SpaceX's Dragon capsule is currently only scheduled to launch humans for a flight to the moon in 2018 (but as of the moment of this printing, details of even that have not yet been released).[9]

While the Falcon Heavy and Dragon combo is enough to take the first crewed missions all the way to the red planet, the spacecraft only seats 4, possibly 6, astronauts. In order to feasibly and sustainably colonize Mars (or any other place), we would need to bring somewhere close to a million people to that planet. This would mean needing an even larger vessel. *Much* larger. Elon Musk knows this, and has proposed beginning work on a new class of rockets.

BFR:

While the Falcon Heavy has the potential to launch satellites, resupply the ISS, or send four to six astronauts to space via the Dragon Capsule, sending small groups won't get humanity further to colonizing Mars. SpaceX has begun research, and plans to begin

---

9 "Crew Dragon". 2018. *Spacex*. http://www.spacex.com/crew-dragon.

development soon, into a new rocket, the BFR (and yes, that does stand for Big Fucking Rocket), capable of carrying 100 people on a cruise-like journey to the red planet.

The development of the first prototypes of the BFR has already begun, and while Musk tends to promise things on a tight schedule and end up with delays, he claims that the rockets could be ready to fly as early as 2019. *"We're actually building that ship right now,"* Musk said in an interview at SXSW in March 2018.. *"I think we'll probably be able to do short flights, short sort of up-and-down flights, probably sometime in the first half of next year."*[10]

While Musk is aware of his reputation for late delivery, he's also known to succeed— even if later than promised. *"People have told me that my timelines historically have been optimistic,"* Musk said. *"So I'm trying to recalibrate to some degree here."* We may not see a BFR ready for travel to Mars in 2022 (as Musk's current timeline indicates), but I have little doubt that we will see one within the next few years, and certainly within the decade.

While SpaceX gets most of the media attention (and is currently the only contract with NASA), it isn't the only private company working towards the goal of sending humans into space. Blue Origin, founded by Jeff Bezos, has been working on the New Shepard, a suborbital rocket to be used for space tourism. The company has also announced the plans to develop the New Glenn, a rocket designed to compete with the Falcon Heavy.

Blue Origin was the first company to ever vertically land a suborbital rocket, the New Shepard, in 2015 (though this rocket didn't actually send anything to orbit). While this is a fantastic feat, Musk was quick to point out the difference between suborbital rockets which visit space, and those which make it to orbit. Of course, this led to a Twitter war between Bezos and Musk, and

---

10 Foust, Jeff. 2018. "Musk Reiterates Plans For Testing BFR". *Spacenews.Com.* http://spacenews.com/musk-reiterates-plans-for-testing-bfr/.

eventually an actual legal battle as SpaceX disputed Blue Origin's attempts to patent the idea of landing on a drone ship. And while everybody loves a little Twitter drama, competition between the companies benefits more than just the internet gossip seekers.

Blue Origin's entire philosophy is much different than that of SpaceX— which happens to be work quickly, blow things up, fail, and continue to innovate. One of Musk's more famous quotes about SpaceX is *"Failure is an option here. If things are not failing, you are not innovating enough."* Blue Origin, by contrast advertises on its website an almost opposite approach:

Driven by our company motto, Gradatim Ferociter or "step by step, ferociously," our incremental development process builds upon each success as we develop groundbreaking spaceflight systems. But we don't just build rockets – we build a culture around methodical innovation and exploration. [11]

Bezos elaborated during the announcement of the New Glenn in 2016, *"Our mascot is the tortoise. We paint one on our vehicles after each successful flight. Our motto is 'Gradatim Ferociter' – step by step, ferociously. We believe 'slow is smooth and smooth is fast.*

"In the long run, deliberate and methodical wins the day, and you do things quickest by never skipping steps. This step-by-step approach is a powerful enabler of boldness and a critical ingredient in achieving the audacious.

"We're excited to give you a preview of our next step. One we've been working on for four years. Meet New Glenn." [12]

---

11 "Our Approach to Technology". 2018. *Blue Origin.* https://www.blueorigin.com/new-shepard.

12 Bergin, Chris, and William Graham. 2016. "Blue Origin Introduce The New Glenn Orbital LV". *NASA Spaceflight.* https://www.nasaspaceflight.com/2016/09/blue-origin-new-glenn-orbital-lv/.

The New Glenn, slated to launch in 2020, will lift off from Cape Canaveral, and plans to compete with other heavy lift launch vehicles, such as SpaceX's Falcon Heavy.

The main thing that Blue Origin is focused on when it comes to this is the development of its engines. Unlike SpaceX, they sell their technology to other aerospace companies, such as United Launch Alliance. According to the company, *"Blue Origin's BE-4 rocket engine is the fastest way to end American dependence on the Russian-made RD-180 engine."*[13]

With all these different approaches to building rockets, a few big questions come to mind. What's the deal with reusability? Why isn't NASA focusing on creating a reusable rocket, when companies like SpaceX and Blue Origin seem to think this is the best way to do things (especially when this seems to be one of the only things they actually can agree upon)?

"The question is cost per pound to lower Earth orbit, cost per pound to the Moon, cost per pound to Mars, and I think it's indisputable that these private sector options, just by their nature, will be more cost-effective than SLS," says Phil Larson, a former space advisor to President Obama and a former representative for SpaceX, *"[It's for] a number of reasons: flight rate, procurement method, and just different ways of doing business."*[14]

The answer is complicated, but the simplest explanation is that it all comes down to organizational politics. For private companies, making a profit is the most important goal — reusability allows them to launch more often and for less money. For NASA, each rocket built employs thousands of people at different contractors

---

13 "Engines". 2018. *Blue Origin*. https://www.blueorigin.com/engines#be-4.
14 Grush, Loren. 2017. "NASA Is Losing The Race To Build A Better Rocket". *The Verge*. https://www.theverge.com/2017/5/10/14886570/nasa-space-launch-system-rocket-ula-blue-origin-spacex.

around the country. If SLS were to be reusable, a large portion of these manufacturing jobs could be eliminated — but NASA employing so many people encourages taxpayer support for the agency and its missions

In the end, having more options when it comes to choosing how to send people to space is always a good thing. *"Having New Glenn, having Falcon Heavy, having SLS — once they're flying, putting them next to each other will be the first time we've had that many capabilities and that many choices,"* Larson explains, *"And the ultimate benefactor of that is the American taxpayer and NASA*

Although we're far from seeing spaceships with warp drives jumping into hyperspace, companies and governments are working together to create the next class of rockets that can take us to Mars, and beyond.

CHAPTER 3

HUMANS MAKE EVERYTHING MORE COMPLICATED

———

Once we reach space, in order to go anywhere meaningful (i.e., far away from the planet), we're going to have to deal with the consequences that traveling through space has on the human body. Fortunately, we're already a step ahead. When it comes to testing the effects of space on the human body, there's no better place than the International Space Station. Located in low Earth orbit, the ISS is the ninth space station to have been inhabited by crews, and has set the record for the longest continuous human presence in space. The space station has been visited by 230 people since its opening in 2000.

Having so many people on the space station – and for such an extensive and unbroken length of time – has allowed us to study and identify some of the main concerns and risks that we need to solve before even attempting a successful Mars mission.

These risks include:

1. Gravity – both living without, and returning to, gravity can cause severe issues
2. Isolation and confinement – the solar system's most incurable case of cabin fever

3. Viral Epidemics – no one wants a Robin Cook novel in space

4. Space radiation – radiation is no joke, and space radiation even more so

5. Distance from Earth – can't turn back around if you forgot to bring your teddy bear

GRAVITY:

Gravity, while something we take for granted here on Earth, is one of the largest sources of problems for astronauts in space. Their bodies must adapt to zero- or low-gravity environments, which can be tough. But one thing most of us don't ever think about is how difficult it can be to re-adapt to *higher*-gravity environments.

When traveling to Mars, for example, colonists would have grown up on Earth, living with a gravitational force of 9.8 m/s^2, then the astronaut would have lived for 18 months in a weightless, zero gravity environment. *Then* the poor soul will land and begin a new life on a surface that has a gravitational force of 3.7 m/s^2. For the human body, transitioning from one gravity field to another is a lot tougher than one would imagine. It affects everything from hand-eye coordination and spatial orientation to balance and locomotion. And all of that is on top of some pretty severe motion sickness.

Without gravity working on your body, your bones lose minerals at the alarming rate of one percent per month. That might not sound too bad until you put it into context — elderly people here on Earth lose 1 percent per *year*. Taking the 18 month journey to Mars would mean risking a loss of more than one sixth of your bone mass — ouch. For those who return to Earth, decreased bone density can cause health problems later in life . . . when you actually *do* get old.

Other health conditions that lack of gravity can cause involve vision problems and an increased risk of developing kidney stones. Often times, medications behave differently in zero-gravity environments, and may not be as effective — or worse, can cause unknown side effects.

This isn't looking too great for us, is it? . . .

What are we doing to prevent and solve these issues?

When it comes to loss of balance and performance, NASA has been creating tests designed to measure astronauts' performance and adaptation to changes in gravity. Research is being done to determine the specific effects of space flight on high-priority exploration mission tasks. Functional tests are developed to represent challenges that crew members may have to solve when starting a mission. These tests are designed identify the key factors that contribute to a decline in performance.

Some of these tests include tool usage, ladder climbing, hatch opening, jumping, obstacle avoidance, and recovery from falls. Astronauts headed for the ISS are tested before (and multiple times after) their stay in order to determine which of the body's systems are most susceptible to decline, and design countermeasures to prevent them. Similar tests are also being done to make sure that astronauts maintain the fine motor skills needed to interact with computers and other sensitive technology in space.[1]

One countermeasure that we are already taking involves copious amounts of exercise. Astronauts on the International Space Station exercise an average of two hours per day, on specially designed equipment to ensure that they are getting the workout they need. Drugs containing bisphosphonates have also shown to be effective in preventing bone loss, and potassium citrate could potentially

---

1 "NASA - Physiological Factors Contributing To Postflight Changes In Functional Performance". 2018. *NASA*. https://www.nasa.gov/mission_pages/station/research/experiments/126.html.

help combat the development of kidney stones (another common problem in space).

NASA also conducts periodic fitness evaluations on all ISS astronauts in order to understand the changes in cardiovascular function that normally occur during spaceflight. They take regular urine samples to monitor astronauts' hydration levels, and NASA is researching into the applications of spinal ultrasounds to monitor back pain.

What about vision issues?

Because of the zero-gravity environment, one of the risks involves bodily fluids slowly moving upwards through the body. This can cause an increased pressure in the eyes, which can cause anything from mild to serious vision problems. Not to worry, though, because there are several different areas of research focusing on solving this problem. One of my favorites involves goggles capable of adjusting both the pressure and refraction around the eye. These are so exciting to me because they can help people here on Earth too.

"The Equinox device has the potential to provide a non-invasive method to treat eye problems affecting astronauts on prolonged space missions," said ophthalmologist Steven Schallhorn, a member of the Vision for Mars advisory team. *"But the spinoff of this technology is even more exciting: it could represent a therapeutic option for patients suffering from glaucoma."*[2]

Another potential solution centers on the idea of using compression cuffs, worn on the thigh, to keep blood in the lower extremities, therefore counteracting the vision changes:

---

2 Wall, Mike. 2015. "New Tech Could Protect Astronauts' Eyes On Mars Mission". *Space.Com.* https://www.space.com/28938-mars-mission-astronaut-vision-tech.html.

"Exposure to weightlessness in space is no picnic: crew members often experience facial puffiness, nasal stuffiness, painful eye movement, dizziness, nausea, and blood rushing to their heads. Russian cosmonauts have used thigh compression cuffs, called the Braslet, in early flight to counter these unpleasant effects. Researchers test a modified Braslet device (Braslet-M) on ISS crew members which show that it is effective in keeping more blood in the legs and could diminish head fluid shift and resulting vision changes."[3]

ISOLATION AND CONFINEMENT:

Have you ever spent 18 months with the same 5 people, locked in a space smaller than most college dorm rooms? (If you have— I would question your life choices). While that doesn't sound ideal for most of us, the astronauts signing up for Mars missions will have to endure the eighteen month journey with little to no privacy. Behavioral issues are inevitable amongst people trapped in a small space together for such long periods of time — no matter how well-trained they are. These issues can include simple things like general boredom and moodiness, loss of morale, and issues with interpersonal interaction, but they can also lead to more serious conditions, such as depression and fatigue.

Because the journey will throw off the body's natural circadian rhythm, astronauts are likely to develop sleep disorders — which aren't helped by the fact that they're living in a small, noisy environment amid the stresses of a rigorous schedule. The lack of a fresh variety of food, while potentially leading to deficiency in nutrition, can also contribute to moodiness.

---

3 "Validation Of On-Orbit Methodology For The Assessment Of Cardiac Function And Changes In The Circulating Volume Using Ultrasound And Braslet-M Occlusion Cuffs, SDTO 17011 U/R". 2017. *NASA*. https://www.nasa.gov/mission_pages/station/research/experiments/356.html.

In addition to all of this, there is a phenomenon called "the third-quarter effect": regardless of how long the mission lasts, morale and motivation are shown to decline three-quarters of the way into the mission. The more confined and isolated humans are, the more likely they are to develop behavioral issues, cognitive conditions, or psychiatric disorders beyond the simple loss of morale.[4] So how do we prevent astronauts from going all Jack Torrance on each other?

NASA already has a rigorous selection process for astronauts who will go to the ISS. Crew members are specially selected and trained to make sure that they will be able to get along during their six month tour on the station. The Mars crew will have an even more rigorous selection process.

Even so, no one is immune to these types of disorders, and so NASA has had to develop other solutions and countermeasures. These solutions range from the complex (such as actigraphy to assess and improve sleep cycles) to the simple (sending astronauts with journals providing a safe place to vent emotions). While not everyone is into journaling, research has shown that journaling does help reduce stress and anxiety.[5][6]

Research is being done into the use of LED lighting to simulate sunlight and help align circadian rhythms, which can improve sleep, alertness, and overall performance.[7] NASA has also

---

4 Putman, John. 2018. "The Space Review: Mars One, The "Third Quarter Effect", And Our Human Journey Into Deep Space". *The Space Review*. http://www.thespacereview.com/article/2683/1.

5 Rosengren, Kurt. 2009. "How Effective Journaling Can Minimize Anxiety". *US News & World Report*. https://money.usnews.com/money/blogs/outside-voices-careers/2009/01/22/how-effective-journaling-can-minimize-anxiety.

6 "Nbehavioral Issues Associated With Isolation And Confinement: Review And Analysis Of Astronaut Journals". 2018. *NASA*. https://www.nasa.gov/mission_pages/station/research/experiments/991.html.

7 "Sleep-Wake Actigraphy And Light Exposure During Spaceflight-Long". 2017. *NASA*. https://www.nasa.gov/mission_pages/station/research/experiments/294.html.

developed a five-minute self-test for astronauts to check for signs of fatigue and assess the impact on their workflow.[8]

VIRAL EPIDEMICS:

Another issue for people traveling to Mars is that the space environment can lead to interesting changes in the characteristics of microbes. According to NASA, up to 95 percent of people on Earth have been infected at some point with the Epstein-Barr virus (EBV), which has been linked with mononucleosis, lymphoma, and other diseases. The virus can be carried for years without side effects, only to be reactivated by stressful events— and launching to space on a rocket traveling at nearly five miles per second and suddenly becoming weightless definitely qualifies as stressful.[9]

Astronauts are also subjected to routine urine testing, not only to check for dehydration, but also to check that there hasn't been any reactivation of viruses (such as EVB) since their arrival on board the ISS. These tests are teaching us how to create more effective prevention methods for future space missions.

Oh! While we're on this microbe train, let's address contamination, because while we can potentially protect ourselves from dormant viruses, we cannot avoid bringing at least a few microbes with us.

"Where humans go, microorganisms follow – even into space. A crew's risk of infectious disease depends on both the concentration and characteristics of microorganisms," Dr. Duane L. Pierson, a scientist working out of NASA's Johnson Space Center, explained in a write-up of his research on the evaluation of microbes on

---

8 "NASA - Solid State Lighting Module, SDTO 15008U". 2017. *NASA*. https://www.nasa.gov/mission_pages/station/research/experiments/651.html.
9 "Space Flight Induced Reactivation Of Latent Epstein-Barr Virus". 2017. *NASA*. https://www.nasa.gov/mission_pages/station/research/experiments/47.html.

board the International Space station.[10] Microorganisms that naturally live on tour body are much more easily transferred from person to person in enclosed habitats, such as on a mission to Mars. Further studies are already being conducted by NASA to understand the effect of space travel on the likelihood of changes in our body's microbiome.[11]

A study conducted on the ISS by Dr. Clarence F. Sams, of NASA's Johnson Space Center, recently concluded that the human immune system is also altered when traveling in space. This can potentially lead to everything from increased susceptibility to illnesses, to the developments of allergies.

"Nine Shuttle crew members gave their blood, sweat, and tears – make that blood, spit, and urine – for this study of immune system changes in space. Samples analyses, done at the Johnson Space Center laboratory, indicate that immune function becomes more compromised as mission workloads grow greater and more complex, which creates more stress. Mission planners need to understand how mission variables and stress levels affect immune responses so they can keep crew members healthy and still meet long-duration mission requirements. Immune system function is particularly a concern for missions exploring the Moon or Mars."[12]

More research is still needed to determine how to best maintain immune system function in space.

---

10 "Surface, Water And Air Biocharacterization - A Comprehensive Characterization Of Microorganisms And Allergens In Spacecraft Environment". 2017. *NASA.* https://www.nasa.gov/mission_pages/station/research/experiments/1033.html.
11 "Study Of The Impact Of Long-Term Space Travel On The Astronauts' Microbiome". 2018. *NASA.* https://www.nasa.gov/mission_pages/station/research/experiments/1010.html.
12 "Validation Of Procedures For Monitoring Crewmember Immune Function - Short Duration Biological Investigation". 2017. *NASA.* https://www.nasa.gov/mission_pages/station/research/experiments/374.html.

SPACE RADIATION:

We'll look into this in more detail in Chapter 4, but radiation is the most dangerous aspect of traveling to Mars, or any other place in the universe, for that matter. Think about it this way: on the space station, which sits just within the Earth's protective magnetic field, astronauts are exposed to levels of radiation that are more than ten times what naturally occur on Earth. However, this is still *much less* than the levels of radiation astronauts on a mission to Mars will encounter.

The first health risk that usually comes to mind when we talk about radiation is cancer, but for astronauts traveling to Mars and beyond, there are many other dangers. Exposure can also lead to degenerative tissue diseases, such as cataracts, cardiac issues, and circulatory issues. The long term effects of radiation can also damage the central nervous system, leading to reduced motor function and behavioral changes. Immediate effects of radiation sickness are not fun either— and they include nausea, vomiting, anorexia, and fatigue — none of which are conducive to a comfortable flight to another planet. It's like motion sickness on crack.

Besides affecting our bodies directly, radiation can also cause changes in the things we bring along with us. Foods and medicines must be stored carefully in order to maintain their nutrient and pharmaceutical values. While your freeze-dried broccoli certainly isn't going to start walking around, ingesting food that has been irradiated is probably a bad idea.

Although treatment of these symptoms can be medically managed, it's better for us all if we can reduce the actual exposure to radiation. Scientists don't have a simple solution to these issues, though shielding, monitoring, and careful procedures currently keep the risk of radiation exposures to acceptable levels on the International Space Station. But before we're ready to travel further, more research will have to be done on how to effectively shield and protect colonists on the journey to the red planet.

One of the biggest issues with researching shielding is that it can be *heavy*. While proven technology is a necessity, and clearly worth the cost, this means that testing new types of shielding in space is impractical when the cost launching a single pound of material to space averages $20,000. So, obviously, testing radiation shielding in space is simply not well advised. Nor is it really ethical to test people's exposure to radiation by actually exposing them to these high levels of radiation. How, then, can we test all of this without actually experiencing it?

NASA has developed advanced computer programs for simulating the effects of different radiation environments, including free space, earth orbit, and even Mars surface. This allows scientists and engineers to study the effects of space radiation on different subjects (such as shielding materials, electronics, or biological systems) without having to actually send the materials there. [13]Using computer models to study the effects of radiation is a great way to prepare for flights, without having to actually fly. They allow scientists to change different variables and predict the outcome almost instantly— rather than waiting on expensive and time-consuming experiments.

DISTANCE FROM EARTH:

I'm well known by friends and family for over packing— I'd pack three pairs of shoes and six outfits for a weekend away if I could, because I definitely might need sandals, sneakers and, *of course,* dress heels. So, when it comes to packing for Mars, I think I'd fit right in. Colonists must pack everything they need, or could possibly ever need, for the 18-month journey to (and subsequent

---

13 "Online Tool For The Assessment Of Radiation In Space". 2018. *OLTARIS.* https://oltaris.nasa.gov/.

stay on) Mars. After all, it's not possible to send a resupply of medicine, drugs or food within any reasonable time frame (or at all really).

The other issue with being so far from Earth is the communication delay. Once on Mars, there is a one-way delay of up to twenty minutes— that means if I were to send you an urgent message, it would take twenty minutes for it to get to you, add time for however long it takes you to reply, and twenty more minutes for me to receive your reply. With the potential for equipment failures and other issues, the first astronauts headed to Mars must be capable of completing the mission on their own, without assistance from a mission control here on Earth.

NASA rigorously trains all astronauts headed to the ISS, so that even if there is not a specialist in an issue, someone up there knows how to solve the problem. Crew selection can help ensure that a variety of astronauts with different strengths are chosen to work together and cover the different challenges of the mission.

This does not mean, however, that we are ready to pack up and go tonight. There are still numerous other studies and tests that must be done before we could ever hope to set foot on Mars. What kinds of future studies are needed, you may ask? Glad you did.

NASA TWIN STUDY

We can begin with the story of Scott and Mark Kelly: they're twin brothers and both are NASA astronauts— in fact, they're the only identical twin astronauts in history. Both men have done multiple space missions — Scott has completed three missions (including a 159-day tour on the ISS), and Mark has completed four space shuttle missions.

NASA wanted to compare what happens to a person's genes in space, so they chose the Kellys to take part in a twin study. For the study, Mark opted to stay on Earth while Scott went to the ISS for the station's first-ever year-long mission. Remember, he'd already done one mission before that, which was back in 2010. On this mission which landed in 2016, however, he was on the station for 340 days, the longest any NASA astronaut has ever stayed in space (though only the fourth longest human spaceflight).

The goal of the mission was to compare the changes to Scott's body with the changes to Mark's body back on Earth. During the mission, he was just performing routine repairs to the station, as well as conducting research. While he was there, he orbited 5,440 times, and he conducted three space walks during the year.

While the results from the twin study are still coming out each day, NASA has collected valuable data that will continue to provide new insights on human spaceflight for years to come. So what do we know so far?

One of the most noticeable changes, Scott grew two whole inches taller! A second change, however, has the potential to be a little more disturbing: Scott appears to have a variety of brand new genes in his body.

For those of you who happen to be keen on biology, Monica Edwards and Laurie Abadie, of NASA's Human Research Strategic Communications, wrote this about the research:

> Whole-genome sequencing showed each twin has hundreds of unique mutations in their genome, more than expected, and some were found only after spaceflight, circulating in the blood as "cell-free DNA". This is thought to be from the stresses of space travel, which can cause changes in a cell's biological pathways and ejection of DNA and RNA. Such actions can trigger the assembly of new molecules, like a fat or protein, cellular degradation; and can turn genes on and off, which change cellular function. Significant responses were found for at least five biological pathways in Scott during his time in space. These responses are important for future missions: hypoxia (likely from lack of

oxygen and high CO_2 levels); mitochondrial stress and increased levels of mitochondria in the blood (indicating damage to the "power plants of cells"); telomere length, DNA damage, and DNA repair (likely from radiation and caloric restriction); collagen, blood clotting, and bone formation (likely from fluid shifts and zero gravity); and hyperactive immune activity (from the new environment). Although 93% of genes' expression returned to normal post-flight, a subset of several hundred "space genes" were still disrupted after return to Earth.[14]

The main takeaway? Scott and Mark Kelly are still identical twins, and Scott's DNA did not fundamentally change. The researchers observed changes in his *gene expression,* which changed as the body reacted to its environment. Only seven percent of the changes in Scott's gene expression had not returned to preflight conditions after six months on Earth.

While we are only at the beginning of understanding how the is the body is affected on the molecular level by spaceflight, the twin studies have given researchers plenty of data to pore over and begin to understand more about the way our bodies react in space.

There were many other studies conducted on the twins, looking at everything from their microbiomes to the thickening of their arteries. The results of these studies will provide answers, and probably some more questions, too, for further investigation. One piece of good news, though, involves vaccines.

Both Mark and Scott were given the flu vaccine three times, each a year apart. For Scott, this was preflight, inflight, and post-flight. The results found that the vaccine was just as effective each time— that's a plus for those who want to stay flu-free on their journey

---

14 Edwards, Monica, and Laurie Abadie. 2018. "NASA Twins Study Investigators To Release Integrated Paper In 2018". *NASA.* https://www.nasa.gov/feature/nasa-twins-study-investigators-to-release-integrated-paper-in-2018.

to Mars. Of course, staying flu-free is a nice goal, but it won't do any good if we get to Mars and have nowhere to go. While we're learning about ways keep our bodies healthy while we travel through space, we've also got to begin planning for how we will survive once we get there. How can we plan for cities in space?

Even in the ancient Sumerian Epic of Gilgamesh (a poem written around 2100 B.C.), there are references to the way our cities should be planned for the better. Though these plans were primitive and had no way of predicting the way that cities in modern times would grow, they served as the foundation upon which modern cities have been built.

Planning for cities on other planets will be a bit like these early plans. While we may currently lack the technology needed, and cannot predict the needs of people generations ahead, we must work to plan towards a future that is exciting and desirable. One thing we know for sure: technology constantly changes, but human values and needs rarely do.

The first colonies on Mars may very well prove to be epic failures, but that should not deter us from looking further out into the universe. Either way, it seems like a prudent idea to learn from our failures here. To begin, we can take a look back on modernist ideas of housing developments – and the failures of housing projects designed during the interwar years in Europe.

LE CORBUSIER AND HIS *PLAN VOISIN*:

In 1922, a young architect named Le Corbusier presented a plan at the Salon d'Automne in Paris. The plan proposed a city of three million inhabitants, built on empty, flat ground. Consisting of three sectors – a business center, a residential area, and a suburb of factories – the plan eliminated the established street style and called for a new style of traffic system to link the city's sectors.

Le Corbusier would come to be one of the most well-known names in architecture, and this design one of the most polarizing topics. While some saw his work as *the* way to design, others saw it as elitist and exclusionary. Two men, Gabriel Voisin and his brother, Charles, were of the former group.

The plan caught their eyes, and the brothers – wealthy manufacturers of automobiles and aircraft – decided to fund a study for the project, asking Le Corbusier to apply the project to the center of Paris. Le Corbusier spent the next few years studying and planning for a presentation of the *Plan Voisin* at the Salon des Arts Décoratifs in 1925.

> *You are under the shade of trees, vast lawns spread all round you. The air is clear and pure; there is hardly any noise. What, you cannot see where the buildings are? Look through the charmingly diapered arabesques of branches out into the sky towards those widely-spaced crystal towers which soar higher than any pinnacle on earth. These translucent prisms that seem to float in the air without anchorage to the ground - flashing in summer sunshine, softly gleaming under grey winter skies, magically glittering at nightfall - are huge blocks of offices.* [15]

- Le Corbusier, *Plan Voisin* (translated)

Sound familiar? Le Corbusier's words bring to mind an image not unlike the renderings of space cities and stations such as those that NASA, SpaceX, and others have proposed for cities on Mars.

The plan proposed demolishing the existing downtown section of Paris (saving a few historic churches and monuments) and replacing it with a rectangular grid of eighteen cross-shaped,

---

15 "Plan Voisin, Paris, France, 1925". 1925. *Fondation Le Corbusier*. http://www. fondationlecorbusier.fr/corbuweb/morpheus.aspx?sysId=13&IrisObjectId=6159& sysLanguage=en-en&itemPos=2&itemCount=2&sysParentName=Home&sysPare ntId=65.

glass office towers, interspersed with green space. An adjacent rectangular space of low-rise residential, governmental, and other buildings, also surrounded by green space, would also be built. The development would highlight the city's modernity, featuring integrated highways, train and subway lines, and even an airport.

Of course, as anyone who has ever been to (or seen pictures of) Paris, you'll know this was never put into place. There were several reasons for this:

- It would erase the culture of downtown Paris, and result in a dramatic gentrification of the city
- The sterile, un-ornamented design was shocking to a generation accustomed to the Art Deco style of the time
- The design, and Le Corbusier himself, conveyed an elitist attitude
- The ideology from which the modernist aesthetic developed was inspired by that of Sigmund Freud, as well as the *Communist Manifesto*
- The plan really only considered able bodied, similar people, rather than a diverse community

Even with all these issues, it doesn't mean that the plan was without merit. The question, though, is: How can we learn from Le Corbusier's failed plans, and apply it to creating a plan for a city in space?

Anthony Flint, a fellow at the Lincoln Institute of Land Policy and author of, *Modern Man: The Life of Le Corbusier*, explains Le Corbusier's mindset: "*He believed in autocratic, top-down planning, where today it is all about a participatory, citizen-oriented process. He embraced the separation of uses and sought to kill the street, when today it is all about the street, a mix of uses, and a human scale.*

"Reactions to this extraordinary man fall into three categories: those who adore him, those who detest him, and those who have no idea who he was." Flint explains, *"People are dug in like Red Sox and Yankees fans; talking about Le Corbusier is a bit like bringing up politics or religion at the Thanksgiving table."* And while many people dislike the man, his work has brought up very important principles to consider.

Flint explains the benefits of looking back at Le Corbusier's work: *"There are fundamental themes in Le Corbusier's career that are quite relevant to the most pressing urban issues before us today."* The most pressing urban issues on Earth today will likely be the most pressing urban issues on Mars (and beyond) tomorrow. Flint tells us, *"The first [of these pressing issues] is his appreciation of scale in planning for the future growth of cities."*

If we restrict the area of urban expansion, the destruction falls on the poor, whose homes are redeveloped and placed out of their price range. This expensive housing becomes out of reach for most people, and pushes people out of their neighborhoods. Le Corbusier carefully considered the way cities would expand, believing that upwards expansion, not outwards, was the solution. When it comes to housing on other planets, we don't have the same land restrictions we have here on Earth. We can develop cities from scratch, from a completely blank slate.

According to Flint, *"The second way today's design professionals can learn from Le Corbusier is by looking at his pioneering thinking in efficient housing design."*[16]

How does this work on a new planet devoid of any human history or culture?

---

16 Flint, Anthony. 2018. "The Hazardous Business Of Celebrating Le Corbusier". *Citylab.* https://www.citylab.com/design/2014/11/the-hazardous-business-of-celebrating-le-corbusier/382584/.

When designing habitats for humans on other planets/moons, it's incredibly important to consider efficiency, while still making the place feel like home. For some people, a super clean, sleek, modern design is the way of the future, but for many, the lack of familiarity will be a deterrent. Looking at Le Corbusier's proven designs can show how to create spaces that are efficient and well-planned without compromising on comfort.

I spoke with designer Bryan Versteeg, who designs space habitats for organizations like Mars One. His insight was quite interesting.

"If you're designing a condominium for here on earth, you know you have the same details that you can look through any Architecture magazine: you see the windows and stairs and fireplaces and doors and all these things that you can just use over again. But if you're drawing a place for Mars, you just don't have the repertoire to work with. You don't have, you know, the library. Same with large space stations. There's just – you know, there hasn't been millions of them done – and so you're forced to innovate at every single step, and I found that to be extremely creatively rewarding and intellectually challenging."

Bryan works day and night to change people's visions for what space living might be like. We talked about the stereotypes that science-fiction has brought in about the ideas of living in space.

"When we talk about space exploration, there's kind of almost two modes of thought that we generally see," Bryan told me. *"One is a very sterile version where everything's just white and clean like a laboratory."* We agreed that most people don't want to live boxed-in, in a white laboratory (though Corbusier might volunteer himself).

The other option?

"Or it's a very dystopic version, where it's like either Mad Max *or a* Blade Runner*, where it's dark and it's gritty, as if, you know,*

everything's a mining camp or something. And ultimately that's not where we live, either."

This is where Bryan's job comes in. He plans out communities that people would actually look at and not only say, "I want to go there!" but, "I can see myself living there."

"I've always wanted to live in space, so the parameters with which I would want to live there are pretty broad," Bryan tells me, *"but my wife has not wanted to live in space. So when I design a place that she looks at and says, 'Okay, I would live there,' I know I've kind of crossed this barrier."*

When it comes to the lifestyle on Mars, Bryan explains, *"I think in the near term it would be perhaps very similar to people who grow up on farms where you spend a lot of the day around agriculture and kind of doing your chores. The bulk of our labor near term will be divided between agriculture and construction."* And while designers like Bryan have begun thinking about life on Mars, that's not what this book is about. Where will we go next?

CHAPTER 4

MOON

———

When I began researching for this book, I wanted to create a guide to where we'll go *after* Mars. You might be thinking that the moon should not belong on this list — haven't we been there already?

While companies like SpaceX are looking to head straight to Mars, many people believe that the moon will be a more practical place for people to test the spacefaring lifestyle. In other words, Mars may be the first colony, but the moon will serve an important role in the way that humanity makes the leap towards becoming a multi-planetary species.

I had a chance to talk with Damian Balla, the lead manufacturing engineer at the University of Southern California's Rocket Propulsion Lab, about the potential places we would go beyond the earth. Damian pointed out that the moon is *"fairly close compared to all the other options – it's like a 3 day journey there."* He also noted that, since we've been there previously, it's not likely to require any huge leaps in technology to do it: *"It's like road tripping out across the U.S. in terms of time. I don't think the moon would really require much technological advancement, which is good."*

Other scientists, like Darby Dyar, a professor of astronomy and geology at Mount Holyoke College, are confident that one day we will have a permanent presence on Earth's moon. *"In my lifetime,"* Dyar says, *"we will establish some kind of permanent station on the moon."* Just how far ahead does "in her lifetime" mean, you might ask?

"Mind you, I plan to live another 50 years!" she exclaimed.[1]

In some senses it is surprising that we don't have a colony on the moon *yet*. In 1959, the U.S. Army created a design that experts today deem to be fairly plausible. The colonization plan, called "Project Horizon," included a nuclear powered fortress built to establish a military presence on the moon before the Soviet Union could do the same.

PROJECT HORIZON

The stated project goal: *"There is a requirement for a manned military outpost on the moon. The lunar outpost is required to develop and protect potential United States interests on the moon; to develop techniques in moon-based surveillance of the earth and space, in communications relay, and in operations on the surface of the moon; to serve as a base for exploration of the moon, for further exploration into space and for military operations on the moon if required; and to support scientific investigations on the moon."*

The Army created a plan for a militarized moon base in 1959, which included the proposed launch of multiple early Saturn rockets. The idea was to create a twelve-man lunar base. The permanent base was predicted to cost $6 billion ($51.5 billion, in today's dollars), and was proposed to become operational in

---

1 Cahill, Pat. 2014. "Colonizing The Moon?". *Solar System Exploration Research Virtual Institute*. https://sservi.nasa.gov/articles/colonizing-the-moon/.

December 1966. Unfortunately (or, perhaps, fortunately) the project never progressed past the feasibility stage.[2]

And not to be outdone by the Army, the U.S. Air Force developed the "Lunex Project." They planned to build a *21-man* underground lunar base, operational by 1968. Sort of brings new meaning to the phrase, "taking the fight outside."

LUNEX PROJECT

Lunex's stated project goal: *"The Lunar Expedition has as its objective manned exploration of the moon with the first manned landing and return in late 1967. This one achievement if accomplished before the USSR, will serve to demonstrate conclusively that this nation possesses the capability to win future competition in technology. No space achievement short of this goal will have equal technological significance, historical impact, or excite the entire world."*

The final plan, which was proposed in 1961, was for a 21-airman underground Air Force base. It was scheduled to become fully operational by 1968, at a total cost of $7.5 billion ($62.6 billion with today's inflation). The goal of the Lunex mission was to make its first lunar landing in 1967, beating the Soviets and demonstrating that America would win all future competition with the USSR.[3]

What made the Lunex vehicle unique was that it was designed to land entirely on the surface of the moon, with all of the astronauts – something that had not yet been accomplished. Incidentally, even though the Lunex Project never came into being, the designs eventually inspired the original plans for Apollo. We must ask

2 "Project Horizon". 1961. https://nsarchive2.gwu.edu/NSAEBB/NSAEBB479/docs/EBB-Moon01_sm.pdf.
3 "Lunar Expedition Plan". 1961. http://www.astronautix.com/data/lunex.pdf.

ourselves, however: Why, in light of all these ambitious plans, has progress on a moon base ceased since the 1970's?

Back in the 1970's, the race to outer space was primarily a military one. The US government was able to spend billions of tax dollars on missions to the moon because public support for NASA was at a high point. By the time the Cold War ended in 1991, we had focused our efforts in other places, and funding for NASA and space exploration dwindled.

We are not on the moon because the Soviet Union was no longer a threat. That's the short of it.

TECHNICAL CHALLENGES TO GOING TO THE MOON:

Of course, this is not to say that setting up bases on the moon is an easy thing without any challenges. And, perhaps, blaming the end of the Cold War *is* a bit too simplistic. Yes, with the waning interest, cuts were made, but those particular cuts were chosen for very practical reasons: setting up a base on the moon is expensive and dangerous, and if there's no real motivation – other than curiosity and pride – then it would naturally be shelved.

But are the challenges so great as to give up entirely? What are these challenges that NASA would face, trying to colonize the moon? There are four main technical issues to overcome: radiation, water, temperatures, and gravity. None of these are impossible to overcome– like I said, the technology exists – but "possible" and "easy" are not necessarily the same thing.

1. Radiation

When it comes to sending people to a place like the moon, radiation is the biggest cause for concern. In physics, radiation is the term for the emission of energy in the form of moving particles or waves. Examples of this include visible light, radio waves, and thermal radiation (heat). But none of these are particularly dangerous (heat *can* be, but only in large quantities).

When you think of *dangerous* radiation here on Earth, you may think of microwave or UV radiation — both of which are types of non-ionizing radiation. These types of radiation, while also being somewhat harmful to the human body, are not the main concern in space.

An ion is just a fancy term for a charged particle, or an atom or molecule with a net electric charge caused by a gain or loss (in this case) of electrons. Ionizing radiation is a type of radiation that can cause other atoms to lose electrons, breaking chemical bonds and creating ions. Examples of this include x-rays, gamma rays, and cosmic rays.

Ionizing radiation occurs in space when atoms accelerate in interstellar space, causing electrons to strip away as these energetic atoms reach the speed of light. Eventually only the nucleus of the atom remains, and that nucleus has so much energy that it is able to knock the electrons out of other atoms as it strikes them.[4]

Sounds violent, right? Molecularly speaking, it is. The effects of this cause damage to human cells, and can lead to cancer and other health problems (sadly, however, they *do not* turn people into giant, green rage monsters . . . pity).

There are three types of ionizing radiation in space:

1. particles trapped in the Earth's magnetic field
2. particles shot into space during solar flares
3. galactic cosmic rays originating outside the solar system

---

4 "NASA Facts: Understanding Space Radiation". 2002. *Spaceflight.Nasa.Gov.* https://spaceflight.nasa.gov/spacenews/factsheets/pdfs/radiation.pdf.

The Van Allen Belts

In 1958, James Van Allen discovered that the same magnetic field protecting us from radiation also traps that radiation and keeps it circling around the earth. Though highly charged, the particles do not have enough energy to escape earth's magnetic field. The two Van Allen belts are nested around earth: the lower belt resting closer to the planet is comprised of highly energetic protons, while the outer belt consists of both protons and electrons. The radiation in these belts poses a risk to any astronauts traveling through them.

What about Apollo— they went to the moon, through these belts, and were fine, right?

NASA worked on a few solutions to this issue— but shielding proved impractical to protect from the lower belt, and some of the other solutions were. . . questionable. One solution, proposed by Van Allen himself, examined the possibility of detonating a nuclear payload in the vicinity of the lower belt. The idea was that the additional radioactive material might be enough to give the particles the extra energy needed to escape. Needless to say, NASA did not actually try this — but in 1962 the United States tested a 1.5 megaton "thermonuclear device" (read: bomb) in a portion of the Van Allen belt and caused the radiation levels to temporarily spike.

By the time NASA was ready to send the first Apollo missions, NASA had determined that the crew would be passing through the belts fast enough that the spacecraft's walls, lined with instrumentation, would be enough to protect the astronauts.[5]

"A lot of people think about the Apollo astronauts, and that they didn't have much protection and were fine," John Lane, an applications scientist with ASRC Aerospace Corp. at Kennedy Space Center,

---

5 Teitel, Amy Shira. 2014. "Apollo Rocketed Through The Van Allen Belts". *Popular Science.* https://www.popsci.com/blog-network/vintage-space/apollo-rocketed-through-van-allen-belts.

told *SPACE.com*. *"But in Apollo, it was a very short mission and a lot of it was basically luck. I'm not sure how they managed to be so lucky, but I don't think you can count on luck on short missions for the future or trips to the planets."*[6]

Basically, NASA did not find a solution to this problem, other than traveling quickly and on trajectories planned to limit exposure and avoid dense areas of radiation. But repeated trips to the moon may still be problematic – we're not sure, honestly, and a crew that shuttles materials and passengers back and forth over the years could, after repeated exposure, develop problems.

This is, of course, the main problem with getting to the moon. Once, there, a new set of problems arises: solar flares and galactic cosmic rays.

Solar Flares

Every once in a while (varying between daily and weekly), our sun releases large amounts of electromagnetic energy. This radiation ranges across the spectrum, and includes everything from radio waves to x-rays, to gamma rays. Luckily, humans here on Earth are protected by our atmosphere and magnetic field. Astronauts on the moon, though, do not have either of these protective measures.

In order to protect from these types of radiation, astronauts on the moon will have to create barriers between themselves and the radiation. Lead is a very effective protectant from these types of radiation, as are thick layers of lunar rubble. We'll explore these ideas later on.

---

6 Malik, Tariq. 2005. "Lunar Shields: Radiation Protection For Moon-Based Astronauts". *Space.Com*. https://www.space.com/658-lunar-shields-radiation-protection-moon-based-astronauts.html.

Galactic Cosmic Rays

Galactic Cosmic Rays are easier to predict than radiation from solar flares, but they're much more difficult to protect against. And while research is being done to determine how to best protect astronauts from cosmic radiation, we're still far from a permanent solution.

Galactic cosmic rays are made up of heavy, high-energy ions traveling at nearly the speed of light. They're able to pass effortlessly through a typical spacecraft or through the skin of an unlucky astronaut. These rays are the dominant source of radiation affecting the ISS, and are considered more hazardous than solar particles (don't worry about the astronauts on the ISS, however: they are protected by both the Earth's magnetosphere and the Van Allen Belts).

One of the methods of protecting from radiation is called passive shielding. If you've ever had an x-ray and covered up with a lead apron, you've experienced passive shielding. The lead in the apron protects your vital organs and absorbs the radiation before it reaches your body. In space, however, creating shielding is much more difficult — the variation in the particles' composition and energy spectra make it difficult to find materials that cover everything. In other words, at the moment, we don't really have any viable options.[7]

2. WATER

Another major challenge with putting settlements on the Moon is that we'd have to build a base close enough to where the water is, *and* create a way to tap into it.

---

7 Case, Daniel. 2016. "Passive Radiation Shielding". *NASA*. https://www.nasa.gov/ directorates/spacetech/strg/nstrf2016/Passive_Radiation_Shielding.

"The moon is a very dry place," says Dr. Darby Dyar. *"That's why it's difficult to imagine living on it."* Dyar further explains, *"We have to understand how water got to the moon, how much is still there, and how hard it would be to extract water for human consumption for a settlement."*[8]

In March 2010, the Chandrayaan-1 lunar probe discovered more than 40 small, permanently darkened craters containing water-ice. Dr Paul Spudis, from the Lunar and Planetary Institute in Houston, estimated there were at least 600 million metric tons of ice held within the impact craters located near the moon's north pole.

"It is mostly pure water-ice," Dr Spudis told the BBC. *"It could be under a few tens of centimetres of dry regolith (lunar soil)."*

The finding of water is a huge step towards creating a viable human settlement on the moon. Water can be used for everything from drinking to creating breathable oxygen, and even synthesizing rocket fuel. This is enormously significant, because, as Dr. Spudis explains, *"Now we can say with a fair degree of confidence that a sustainable human presence on the moon is possible. It's possible using the resources we find there."*[9]

Of course, that brings up another important question: if there is water on the moon, *who owns it?*

The Outer Space Treaty of 1967

Formally titled, *The Treaty on Principles Governing the Activities of States in the Exploration and Use of Outer Space, including*

8 Cahill, Pat. 2014. "Colonizing The Moon?". *Solar System Exploration Research Virtual Institute*. https://sservi.nasa.gov/articles/colonizing-the-moon/.
9 Rincon, Paul. 2010. "Ice Deposits Found At Moon's Pole". *BBC News*. http://news.bbc.co.uk/1/hi/sci/tech/8544635.stm.

the Moon and Other Celestial Bodies, the treaty is the basis of international space law. The treaty was signed by the United States, the Soviet Union, and the United Kingdom in 1967, and as of 2018 has been ratified by 105 countries.

The treaty outlined the rules for space, including a ban on nuclear weapons, and an agreement that all activities in space would be for peaceful purposes. The Outer Space Treaty also prevents individual nations from claiming ownership of land or resources on the moon or other celestial bodies.

The issue with the treaty arises when private citizens and companies enter the arena. Technically, companies and individuals are not subject to the Outer Space Treaty. There are companies, like LunarLand, which has been selling acres of land on the moon to individuals around the world since 1980. When it comes time to actually create settlements on the moon, there could be potential issues with the legal standing of these lunar deeds, and the ownership and use of resources, such as water.

3. TEMPERATURES

Since the Moon has no atmosphere, the temperatures swing wildly between day and night. Temperatures during the day reach up to 240°F (116°C) but drop to -279°F (-173°C) during the long nights. Since a full day on the moon lasts just under 656 hours, people on the moon would experience two weeks of extreme heat during the lunar day, followed by two weeks of cold, dark night. Luckily, temperature is one of the easier problems to solve.

Bases on the moon will have to be built to withstand thermal stresses and heat expansion, as well as provide adequate insulation for the inhabitants. The solution to this issue may be to dig into tunnels on the surface, or to use lunar soil to build insulated structures where people can shelter during the harsh heat and cool. Bases could also be built near the poles of the moon, where the night cycle is slightly shorter.[10]

4. GRAVITY

When it comes to visiting the moon, the idea of a gravity being 83.3% less than that of the earth might sound like fun. Who wouldn't to play a round of golf, like Alan Shepard did in 1971, where the balls travel for miles and miles?

In reality, however, the lack of gravity can lead to issues during prolonged stays. Residents on the moon would have to maintain strict exercise schedules, similar to those on the ISS, in order to maintain bone density and muscle mass when they return to earth. While people vacationing or visiting for a short time won't be as affected, long-term lunar residents will have difficulties when returning to Earth without following exercise routines.

Though these challenges need to be solved – and most of them have been – there are plenty of reasons why we should be going to the moon. As we've noted, in fact, there are many who would argue that we must go to the moon *before* we could ever hope to colonize Mars.

WHY THE MOON WOULD MAKE A GOOD COLONY

Even with all of these challenges, we've been there, done that and bought the t-shirt when it comes to the moon. But while there's not an extensive amount for us to learn *about* the moon, what the moon can still teach us about living in space is even more valuable. If we plan to move past Mars, setting up a colony on the moon will be a great way to learn how humans react to space travel, to

10 Allison, Peter. 2015. "This Is Why Lunar Colonies Will Need To Live Underground". *Bbc.Com*. http://www.bbc.com/future/story/20151218-how-to-survive-the-freezing-lunar-night.

understand low-gravity living, and be a relatively low-risk way to observe human life in an increased radiation environment.

We'll most likely see the moon used in one of three main use cases:

- As a staging ground for equipment and people to travel to other celestial bodies.
- As a tourist destination for humans.
- Energy and resource mining.

The Moon as a Staging Ground.

One of the mostly likely uses of a moon colony or settlement is the equivalent of a space-pit stop, according to some scientists, like NASA's Chris McKay. He believes that the moon is the best option as a sort of stepping-stone to the rest of the solar system. *"If we ever have a human base on another world I would bet it would be the moon first,"* McKay explained to Futurism. *"Being so close, and constantly so close, is really a killer advantage over Mars, or asteroids, or anywhere else."*[11]

The advantage of going to the Moon is that its proximity allows for it to be used as a low-stakes test case. We have a lot to learn before we're ready to colonize other places, and going in blind isn't going to do us much good. Experiments can be run on the moon to test the effects of a low-gravity environment on everything, from growing vegetables and raising animals, to perfecting low-gravity manufacturing processes and mining techniques.

The moon is close enough to Earth that if something were to go wrong, or supplies were to run low, we would be able to send help within a matter of days. The colony on the moon could be used to test workflows, habitats, and living conditions without

---

11   Jones, Brad. 2017. "New Discovery Raises Hope For Human Colonization Of The Moon". *Futurism*. https://futurism.com/discovery-hope-colonization-moon/.

the strings of a one way mission attached. Mars, which is often proposed as the site of a first settlement, does not compare with this accessibility.

Director of the European Space Agency (ESA), Johann-Dietrich Woerner, explains. *"We should look to the future beyond the International Space Station."* He continues, *"We should look for a smaller spacecraft in low-Earth orbit for microgravity research and I propose a Moon village on the far side of the Moon.*

"The Americans are looking to go to Mars very soon – and I don't see how we can do that – before going to Mars we should test what we could do on Mars on the moon."

Why the far side?

This side of the moon is often called the "dark" side, though it receives the same amount of light as the near side. The moon is tidally locked with earth, so the far side is never seen from here, but it has the same day and night cycles as the near side. Woerner explains that having a base on the far side would allow for us to build radio telescopes that could look further into space than ever before, because the moon would shield them from background radiation-chatter broadcasts from earth. Building a base on the far side would also mean that astronauts would need a satellite relay system to communicate with earth, which would be important to develop as we venture further from the earth.

"A Moon village shouldn't just mean some houses, a church and a town hall," says Woerner. *"This Moon village should mean partners from all over the world contributing to this community with robotic and astronaut missions and support communication satellites."*[12]

12 Hollingham, Richard. 2015. "Should We Build A Village On The Moon?". *Bbc. Com.* http://www.bbc.com/future/story/20150712-should-we-build-a-village-on-the-moon.

The Moon as a Resort

In 2016, Woerner announced that the ESA was planning to create a lunar village in the not-too-distant future. The village would be designed with the partial intention of giving citizens of Earth the potential to vacation on the moon.

"Our work is to do research, science and development, but I'm quite sure — as we saw happening here on Earth — that tourism will follow exploration," he says. *"It's not out of reach, as it was not out of reach in the late '50s of last century to go to the moon,"* he says. *"Of course, there are many developments necessary for that. But I think from a feasibility point of view it is feasible, it is visionary, it is demanding. In general, it should be possible."*[13]

Governments like the ESA are focused on getting humans to the Moon to conduct research, but private companies are in the race to make a profit. In a way, we can think of the potential for a base on the moon to be, not strictly a living destination, but a place to vacation. There is no reason why there cannot be a tourist village on the Moon. There are currently no laws preventing private companies from making it to the moon and creating settlements of their own.

The existence of a lunar resort could potentially be accomplished by private companies after research bases are established by governmental organizations. There are companies already working on space tourism, such as Space Adventures, which has sold two tickets to orbit the moon, sent multiple tourists to the International Space Station, and offers us mortals the deal of a lifetime — a trip on a zero gravity flight for just under five grand (okay, maybe not exactly a sale at the grocery store, but still comparatively cheap).

---

13 Spector, Julian. 2015. "How To Build A City On The Moon". *Citylab*. https://www.citylab.com/equity/2015/08/how-to-build-a-city-on-the-moon/400454/.

Another key player is Richard Branson's Virgin Galactic — which has already sold tickets to send people on space flights, though they have not yet launched a paying customer. Blue Origin also has plans for using its New Glenn rocket to launch space tourists . . . at some point in the future.

Why Vacation on The Moon?

It might seem crazy to say that people will want to go to a place with two weeks of constant darkness, temperatures swinging across a spectrum of hundreds of degrees, and levels of radiation that can cause cancer, but people are already willing to pay exorbitant amounts for the chance to do so. Space Adventures boasts on its website about the two private citizens who will take a journey around the moon in flight-proven Russian space vehicles, accompanied by a professional cosmonaut. SpaceX has also announced that they have a contract to send two unnamed customers into lunar orbit via the Crew Dragon and Falcon Heavy. Though the customers of both missions remain unnamed, they have paid a significant deposit for a trip costing upwards of a hundred million dollars.[14]

The moon is our gateway to outer space. It's someplace that almost every kid (ok— maybe just me, and my fellow space nerds) dreams of visiting. Especially if we can get the costs to visit down to something comparable with a trip to Disney, the thrill of launching to space and taking a visit to the moon alone will be enough to draw many people to take the trip.

"In our genes there is something beyond just practical applications," Woerner says of the plans to colonize the moon. *"We like to*

---

14 Adventures, Space. 2018. "Circumlunar Mission - Space Adventures". *Space Adventures.* http://www.spaceadventures.com/experiences/circumlunar-mission/.

discover, to pioneer – this is humankind and this is what brings us into the future." [15]

If you think of it like a glorified road trip, imagine the types of activities:

- Visits to historical sites, such as the Apollo 11 landing site.

- Extreme hiking and exploring the craters and mountains on the surface of the moon.

- Breathtaking views of the earth and the stars.

While a Mars landing can reasonably be expected within the next few decades, the timeline for a tourist destination on the moon is slightly more difficult to predict. If governmental organizations, like the ESA, follow through on plans to build a permanent lunar base, private companies and tourism will be quick to follow.

It might seem like a stretch to believe that just because there are astronauts on the moon, people will want to pay to go there, but that's exactly what happened with the International Space Station. In 2001, just *one year* after the first astronauts arrived at the ISS, the first paying tourist was sent to the ISS. American engineer and multimillionaire Dennis Tito paid $20 million to become the first space tourist, hitching a ride in the Russian Soyuz TM-32 mission.

Out of a total of 277 people have visited the ISS, seven of them have been paying tourists. All of them were launched from the Russian Space Agency, sold through Space Adventures. The ISS tourists were generally on board the station during the one to two week crew changeover, and were all sent up aboard the three-seat Soyuz spacecraft.

---

15 Hollingham, Richard. 2015. "Should We Build A Village On The Moon?". *Bbc. Com.* http://www.bbc.com/future/story/20150712-should-we-build-a-village-on-the-moon.

Resource Mining

One resource that earth is lacking somewhat – and one the moon has in abundance – is helium-3. Now, to understand *why* we might want to mine helium-3 on the moon, I'll have to explain a little bit about nuclear reactions. Bear with me; it's actually interesting stuff.

Currently, nuclear power plants produce heat by harnessing the energy of some kind of nuclear reaction (what kind depends on the reactor). The heat turns water into steam, which drives a turbine and produces electricity. Nuclear fission reactors are used to create a reaction in which the nuclei of uranium atoms are split apart — creating energy, but also creating radioactive waste which cannot be disposed of and is usually buried in repositories away from populated areas (okay for people, but not good for the environment as a whole).

There is another type of nuclear reaction, called a fusion reaction, in which atoms are combined rather than split apart. In current nuclear fusion reactors, two hydrogen isotopes (tritium and deuterium) are combined to create a helium atom plus a neutron. The neutrons released by this type of fusion reaction are difficult to contain, and lead to significant energy loss. In order to create a more efficient reaction, helium-3 and deuterium could be fused to create a "normal" helium atom and a proton, which would provide a much more efficient form of nuclear power with no radiation or waste.

One of the main reasons we don't have a helium-3 fusion reactor working yet is that this isotope is extremely rare here on earth. However, the isotope is actually released by the sun's solar winds, and while earth's atmosphere prevents it from arriving here, the moon soaks the stuff right up. It's been estimated that the surface of the moon contains nearly 1,100,000 metric tons [that's the British spelling!] of helium-3. If scientists here on earth were to perfect a helium-3 fusion reactor, just 25 tons of the stuff could power all of the United States — for a whole year.

If all this were to work, the net value of a single ton of helium-3 would come out to about $3 billion— making a trip to the moon economically practical.[16]

Who will go?

Competition with the USSR was the main driving factor for the US Government to make it to the moon back in the 1960's. McKay, among others, believes that this spirit of competition is necessary if we're going to make it back to the moon and beyond. *"The U.S. is unlikely to have a large activity on the moon or Mars if it is the only actor involved,"* McKay told Futurism. *"Why play 'king of the mountain' if you're the only one on the mountain[?] However if private groups or other nations are [planning] to go to the moon and/or Mars then the U.S. will want to be involved and in fact to be in the lead."*[17]

So far, there are only a handful of players on the field. However, that handful is a fairly large one, and includes some major league players such as the United States, Japan, and Europe. On the other hand, while keeping up with the competition is a likely motivator for these countries to develop technology, when it comes to the actual settlement of a moon base, many believe that cooperation, not competition, will be the key to success. As an example, the European Space Agency has been open about its goal for an international cooperative effort to get back to the moon.

"We should have international cooperation, without any limitations, with any countries of the world," said Woerner. *"We have enough Earthly problems between different nations – space can bridge these Earthly problems and the Moon seems to be to be a good proposal."*

---

16 Barnatt, Christopher. 2016. "Helium-3 Power". *Explainingthefuture.Com.* http://www.explainingthefuture.com/helium3.html.
17 Jones, Brad. 2017. "New Discovery Raises Hope For Human Colonization Of The Moon". *Futurism.* https://futurism.com/discovery-hope-colonization-moon/.

Woerner continues: *"Isolating a country is not the right way, a much better solution is to find ways to cooperate in space to strengthen ties between humans on Earth."*

While the idea of a moon base is currently just a proposal, there are a few different ideas on how it could be built. These ideas include everything from 3D Printing, to subterranean (actually, I guess it would be sub*lunar*ean) bases.

3D Printing with Lunar Materials

The moon is coated in a thick layer of dirt and rubble known as regolith. The ESA has been researching into plans for a base that looks kind of like a hobbit hole. Robots would travel to the moon and use lunar regolith and special enzymes to create a cement-like 3D printed lunar base. On Earth, 3D printing has already been used to build homes in record time, and the technology is quickly evolving.

"Terrestrial 3D printing technology has produced entire structures," said Laurent Pambaguian, the head of the project for ESA. *"Our industrial team investigated if it could similarly be employed to build a lunar habitat."*

"3D printing offers a potential means of facilitating lunar settlement with reduced logistics from Earth," added Scott Hovland, a member of ESA's human spaceflight team. As exciting as it sounds, though, what, exactly would this mean?

Robots would be sent with inflatable habitats, which could then be printed over using the lunar regolith.

"As a practice, we are used to designing for extreme climates on Earth and exploiting the environmental benefits of using local, sustainable materials," Xavier De Kestelier, of Foster + Partners Specialist Modelling Group, explained in an article by the European Space Agency. *"Our lunar habitation follows a similar logic."* The use of

lunar materials would eliminate the need to send materials from earth, which saves time and money.

How would it actually work to 3D print a structure on the moon?

"First, we needed to mix the simulated lunar material with magnesium oxide. This turns it into 'paper' we can print with," Monolite founder Enrico Dini explained to the ESA. *"Then for our structural 'ink' we apply a binding salt, which converts material to a stone-like solid. Our current printer builds at a rate of around 2 m per hour, while our next-generation design should attain 3.5 m per hour, completing an entire building in a week,"* Dini concluded.[18]

Lava Tunnels

The moon is full of craters and ancient lava tunnels. These underground caves would make an ideal place for moon bases, as they're naturally very strong and protected from radiation and asteroid impact.

"We've known about these locations that were thought to be lava tubes ... but their existence has not been confirmed until now," said Junichi Haruyama, a senior researcher at the Japan Aerospace Exploration Agency, in October 2017. *"It's important to know where and how big lunar lava tubes are if we're ever going to construct a lunar base,"* continues Haruyama. *"But knowing these things is also important for basic science. We might get new types of rock samples, heat flow data and lunar quake observation data."*

Haruyama believes that these natural lava tubes *"might be the best candidate sites for future lunar bases, because of their stable thermal conditions and potential to protect people and instruments from micrometeorites and cosmic ray radiation."* While this is an exciting discovery, there is a lot to learn before the details of living

18 "Building A Lunar Base With 3D Printing". 2013. *European Space Agency*. http://www.esa.int/Our_Activities/Space_Engineering_Technology/Building_a_lunar_base_with_3D_printing.

in one of these tubes can be flushed out. *"We haven't actually seen the inside of the cave itself so there are high hopes that exploring it will offer more details,"* Haruyama said.[19]

With many possibilities for bases to be built, it's not necessarily a question of if we will establish a presence on the moon, but a question of how it all plays out. While it may not be the ideal *permanent* living space, the moon will be an important part of our journey out into the universe. With only a few hurdles left to jump, though, we may very well see an operational moon base in our lifetime.

19 McCurry, Justin. 2017. "Discovery Of 50Km Cave Raises Hopes For Human Colonisation Of Moon". *The Guardian.* https://www.theguardian.com/science/2017/oct/19/lunar-cave-discovery-raises-hopes-for-human-colonisation-of-moon.

CHAPTER 5

TITAN

"If you were in the outer solar system and you had to make an emergency landing, go to Titan," says NASA astrobiologist Chris McKay.[1]

Titan is Saturn's largest moon, and is tidally locked with the ringed planet — just like our own moon here on Earth. While Titan is much larger than our moon, it has lower gravity than that of our own moon (this is due to its lower density — in case you were wondering). And while most moons have very little, if any, protective atmosphere, Titan has an atmospheric pressure 1.5 times that of Earth's. This makes Titan a much more interesting place for scientists (and those who dream of living in space) as its thick atmosphere of nitrogen and methane could protect settlers from radiation.

HOW DO WE KNOW SO MUCH ABOUT TITAN?

In 1997, NASA, the ESA, and the Italian Space Agency launched the Cassini-Huygens mission on a journey to the previously

---

1 Castro, Joseph. 2015. "What It Would Be Like To Live On Saturn's Moons Titan And Enceladus". *Space.Com.* https://www.space.com/28786-living-on-saturn-moons-titan-enceladus.html.

unexplored Saturn system. The spacecraft arrived at Saturn in 2004, and began its detailed study of the planet, its rings, and its moons. In 2005, Cassini delivered the Huygens probe to Titan. The Cassini spacecraft performed many more flybys of Saturn's largest moon, gathering immense amounts about its weather, geography, and climate.

When it was realized that the moons of Saturn would potentially host life, which could be contaminated by microbes hitching a ride on the spacecraft, the decision was made to end Cassini's visit with a final dive into Saturn's atmosphere. In what became known as the spacecraft's "Grand Finale," Cassini dipped between Saturn's rings and headed directly for the planet, transmitting information back to earth until it burned up in the planet's atmosphere.[2]

While the end of the mission was bittersweet to many, it left behind a rich legacy and fundamentally altered the way we think about Saturn and its moons. It's (literal) crash and burn allowed scientists to explore the atmosphere of Saturn, and the mission will live on as the data it has gathered continues to provide insights for decades to come.

Professor Simon Green, who helped develop the Huygens lander, explains the groundbreaking nature of the mission:

The Cassini-Huygens mission has transformed our understanding of the second largest planet in our solar system, Saturn, with its vast ring system and its unique moons. Landing on Titan revealed a cold, but surprisingly Earth-like landscape, shaped by the flow of

2 "Cassini Legacy: 1997-2017 : Why Cassini Mattered". 2018. *Jet Propulsion Laboratory*. https://saturn.jpl.nasa.gov/mission/grand-finale/why-cassini-matters/.

methane rather than water [...] The scientific legacy of the mission will extend long beyond its fiery end in the clouds of Saturn.[3]

Those who dream of living on Titan have Cassini-Huygens to thank, and because of the data collected, we have an idea of what life there might actually might be like. Imagine waking up, putting on a heated coat, and taking a stroll through a beautiful rocky desert. You climb a hill and turn the temperature down slightly on your jacket, spread your arms, and take a leap off. The fabric between your arms acts like wings, allowing you to glide across the landscape. You catch glimpses of shimmering lakes and modular settlements. You land gently, in a way that reminds you of gliding to the bottom of a swimming pool after making a cannonball, and trek a bit further to the large greenhouse where you work.

Human colonists might one day arrive on Titan, if we can solve three main technical challenges:

1. Travel time
2. Temperature
3. An annoyingly distinct lack of oxygen

Let's address each of these challenges once at a time.

TRAVEL TIME

It took the Cassini-Huygens probe seven years to travel to Titan from Earth. Voyager 1 made the journey past Saturn in just over three years, and Voyager 2 passed the planet just around four years after launch. The difference in travel time is based on the goal of the mission. The Voyager missions both flew past Saturn, without

---

3 Radowitz, John. 2018. "20-Year Cassini Mission Is About To End With A Death Plunge Into Saturn". *The Independent.* https://www.independent.co.uk/news/science/cassini-grand-finale-images-nasa-saturn-mission-findings-huygens-enceladus-titan-a7948076.html.

need for deceleration. Cassini had to slow down and orbit the moon, allowing for Huygens to actually make a landing.

The need to decelerate is what slows the travel time the most. Let's take a little look at the physics behind this. You may remember Newton's Laws of Motion from high school physics:

- **Newton's First Law:** A body will remain at rest or in motion in a straight line unless acted upon by a force.

- **Newton's Second Law:** Acceleration of an object is dependent on the forces acting upon it and it's mass. If the net force is increased, the acceleration is increased. For a given net force, the more mass a particle has, the less acceleration it has. This is described using the equation: Force = Mass x Acceleration.

- **Newton's Third Law:** To every action there is an equal and opposite reaction.

Rockets launch and accelerate according to Newton's Third Law - fuel is spent, and the equal and opposite reaction pushes the rocket to accelerate away from Earth. Once the spacecraft reaches the vacuum of space, and is not near any large gravitational force, Newton's First Law applies, and it will remain in motion, heading towards its destination. The rocket does not need to fire its engines once it reaches a coasting speed, and so a spacecraft carrying humans to Titan could accelerate and then coast until it reaches Titan. But, Newton's laws (and all the other laws of physics) still apply once the spacecraft arrives at its destination. What does this mean? Fuel is needed to slow the spacecraft down in order to orbit, and even more fuel is needed to send the lander to the surface.

The faster the spacecraft is traveling, the more fuel will be needed to slow it down on the other end. More fuel to use later means a heavier mass, and more fuel required to accelerate from Earth. With missions like Voyager, which planned to pass by Saturn and continue on its path, less fuel was needed to decelerate, allowing for a greater travel speed (and, thus, less time). Of course, with all of this fuel being used, one very important question is: How much does rocket fuel cost?

For the Space Shuttle missions, NASA reported that it paid 98 cents per gallon for hydrogen, and 87 cents per gallon for oxygen. This might sound cheap until you consider that filling the tank of the space shuttle requires 384,071 gallons of liquid hydrogen and 141,750 gallons of liquid oxygen. Along with other propellants, such as hydrazine, monomethylhydrazine, and dinitrogen tetroxide, the total cost came in at more than $1.3 million in fuel. That might make you feel a little better next time you spend $50 filling your car at the gas station!

Rocket fuel isn't just expensive in the monetary sense. Fuel is heavy, with one gallon of liquid oxygen weighing in at 4.322 kg, and liquid hydrogen weighing in at 0.268 kg per gallon. NASA reported the total weight of propellants in the space shuttle to be more than 729,005 kg (1,607,185 lbs)[4]. That alone is a lot of mass to lift off the ground, but it is complicated further, of course, by the fact that as you lift the rocket the mass decreases (because the fuel burns, right?).

Glad I'm not a rocket scientist.

One solution to the issue of fuel is refilling the spacecraft bound for Titan once it is in Earth's orbit. The rocket would launch from earth with just enough propellant to get it to orbit, and dock with a fueling station, where it will be filled and prepared for the journey. This would decrease the amount of fuel needed for liftoff and, by extension, would decrease the total fuel needed to make the journey to Titan. Of course, when talking about fuel

---

4 "Space Shuttle Use Of Propellant And Fluids". 2006. *NASA*. https://www.nasa.gov/centers/kennedy/pdf/167433main_Propellants08.pdf.

and speed, the most important reason to go fast is to get people to their destination as quickly as possible.

With human spaceflight, time is really important. The more time humans are traveling, the more time they are exposed to harmful space radiation. In order for humans to safely travel to Titan, we would need to either drastically improve the quality of radiation shielding, or cut down the travel time needed to reach the moon.

Astronauts on the ISS are only allowed to stay for 6 months, and they're below the Van Allen Belts, protected from the worst of space radiation. The journey to Earth's moon, which is just 3 days long, is still considered risky. Astronauts traveling to Titan would be exposed to a much larger amount of radiation than those on the ISS or traveling to our own moon, and for a *much* longer period of time.

No bueno.

Some ideas for protecting the astronauts on their journey to Titan include everything from creating magnetic fields on the spacecraft (requires a lot of power), coating the entire spacecraft in lunar rubble (never been done before, and would require some sort of moon base – *but* . . . the spaceship would resemble The Thing, so that'd be cool), or simply building a spacecraft with a very, very thick hull (heavy and expensive).

So far, there aren't really any good options. However, for the sake of argument, let's assume we figure it out. Does that mean we're ready to go? Not exactly. Even assuming we can solve these challenges of travel, there will be additional challenges for colonists once they land on Titan.

Temperature

The average temperature on Titan is -179 degrees Celsius (-290 F). That makes living in the coldest places on Earth, where the lowest temperatures reach -55C, sound downright balmy. Luckily, it's a lot warmer on Titan than in open space (the temperature of particles in space is much, much, colder at 270.45C (-454.81F), and we've already got space suits capable of protecting us from freezing in open space.

For humans to survive on Titan, we will need to develop clothing that is something of a mix between traditional space suits and the clothing worn in the arctic. Fortunately, the technology for both already exists, and finding a crossover won't be the biggest hurdle for surviving on Titan.

Atmosphere

The atmosphere on Titan is made up of 98.4% nitrogen, with the remaining percentage comprised of hydrogen and methane. The lack of breathable oxygen in the atmosphere sounds like a major turn off, but the good news is that there is water below the surface of Titan. This means that breathable O_2 can be extracted from the water, a process that is already being done on the ISS through a process called electrolysis.

Electrolysis is a method of separating elements using an electric current. On the ISS, this process is used in the Oxygen Generator System (OGS), which is a major part of the life-support systems on the station. The way the OGS works is that it collects water from various sources on board, including condensation, wastewater – yes, even urine – and converts that water into breathable oxygen and usable hydrogen.

Now, as many of you are no doubt aware, plants naturally produce oxygen as a waste product, similar to the way we produce carbon dioxide as a waste product. So, naturally, the question most of us would ask is why plants can't just be used for this process.

Jay Perry, an aerospace engineer at NASA's Marshall Space Flight Center, is working on the Environmental Control and Life Support Systems (ECLSS) project. He explains: *"Chemical-mechanical* systems," such as those used on the OGS, *"are much more compact, less labor intensive, and more reliable than a plant-based system."*

Perry doesn't rule out the possibility of a plant based life support system for future generations, but notes that there are numerous leaps to be made before it is ready. *"A plant-based life support system design is presently at the basic research and demonstration stage of maturity and there are a myriad of challenges that must be overcome to make it viable."*[5]

Though this technology might be developed some day, because we have chemical processes to do the same thing at a lower cost, we're better off focusing our plant research on how to grow food – a problem that will always exist, everywhere.

HOW *DO* WE GROW FOOD IN SPACE?

In the movie *The Martian,* directed by Ridley Scott and based on the book by Andy Weir, astronaut Mark Watney is stranded on Mars. One of the first challenges he has to face is the lack of food. In the movie, he engineers a device that distills water from the air and grows potatoes in Martian soil — using nutrients from his own poop. Thankfully, astronauts bound for Titan will have a few more options when it comes to how they'll grow and prepare their food.

On the International Space Station, astronauts are growing plants using a special Vegetable Production System, "Veggie", which provides a self-sufficient and sustainable food source as well as a source of recreation and relaxation. The way Veggie works is by providing seeds a sense of direction. An astronaut will essentially glue a seed into a wicking material, making sure that the roots will point downwards and the stem upwards. The wick is then

5 Barry, Patrick L. 2000. "Breathing Easy On The Space Station | Science Mission Directorate". *NASA Science Beta.* https://science.nasa.gov/science-news/science-at-nasa/2000/ast13nov_1.

inserted into a "plant pillow," which is a bag of dirt, fertilizer, and nutrients.[6] The pillows are placed under an LED light, which gives the plants the energy needed to grow, as well as a further sense of direction. Because *no one* wants discombobulated plants.

So far, Veggie has been used to grow red romaine lettuce, cabbage, mizuna (an arugula-like lettuce), and zinnia flowers. Growing salads is just a start for astronauts on the ISS, and more complex plants are in line to be tested next. The Zinnia flowers provided insights into the way flowering plants will be able to grow in zero gravity and serve as a stepping stone towards things like tomatoes.[7]

Dr. Gioia Massa, the NASA payload scientist for Veggie, explained the importance of taking plants to space: *"The farther and longer humans go away from Earth, the greater the need to be able to grow plants for food, atmosphere recycling and psychological benefits. I think that plant systems will become important components of any long-duration exploration scenario."*

Luckily, research into how to grow food more productively and cheaply will not just benefit space colonists — it will also help people here on Earth *"We hope to increase the amount and type of crop in the future, and this will allow us to learn more about growing plants in microgravity,"* Massa continued. *"We have upcoming experiments that will look at the impacts of light quality on crop yield, nutrition and flavor, both on Earth and in space."*[8]

Of course, growing food isn't all there is to eating. Salads will get old very quickly, and while we may still have a lot to learn

6 Foley, Katherine. 2016. "How Do Astronauts Grow Plants In Space?". *Quartz.* https://qz.com/599928/how-do-astronauts-grow-plants-in-space/.
7 Meggs, Lori. 2010. "Growing Plants And Vegetables In A Space Garden". *NASA.* https://www.nasa.gov/mission_pages/station/research/10-074.html.
8 Herridge, Linda. 2017. "Crew Members Sample Leafy Greens Grown On Space Station". *NASA.* https://www.nasa.gov/mission_pages/station/research/news/meals_ready_to_eat.

about growing food on Titan, what will we do about preparing it? With all the work of building a colony, the first colonists on Titan probably won't have much time to cook or bake (and with the difference in gravity, pressure, and temperature, baking on Titan would probably be somewhat of a nightmare — I definitely wouldn't want to be the one translating that recipe). So, what *will* preparing a meal on Titan look like?

Colonists will probably use 3D printing technology to prepare their meals. Research is already being done by food scientists here on Earth, and there are already printers capable of making everything from stuffed pasta and pizza to chocolate and pastries. Some experts even believe that the grocery stores of the future could contain "food cartridges" with a much longer shelf life than traditional ingredients. While intended for use on Earth — the application of this technology to the space program would greatly benefit those headed to Titan.

Hod Lipson, a professor of mechanical engineering at Columbia, has developed a prototype printer, which fabricates nutrition bars and simple pastries. Lipson believes that the technology could be used to supplement a person's diet and supply them with customized meals, suited to their own individual needs. He explains, *"Food printing could allow consumers to print food with customized nutritional content, optimized based on biometric and genomic data."* Lispon continued, *"So instead of eating a slice of yesterday's bread from the supermarket, you'd eat something baked just for you on demand. This may be the missing link between nutrition and personal medicine, and the food that's on your table."* [9] When it comes to feeding colonists on Titan, foods customized and baked on demand sound pretty good (imagine a real-life version of the Nutri-Matic machine in *Hitchhikers Guide*).

---

9 Wiggers, Kyle. 2017. "From Pixels To Plate, Food Has Become 3D Printing'S Delicious New Frontier". *Digital Trends*. https://www.digitaltrends.com/cool-tech/3d-food-printers-how-they-could-change-what-you-eat/.

For Lipson, who has worked on many different types of 3D printers, printing food is especially exciting. As he puts it, *"It touches on something that's very basic to our lives. We've been cooking forever, but if you think about it, while technology and software have wormed their way into almost every aspect of our lives, cooking is still very, very primitive—we still cook over an open flame, like our ancestors millennia ago. So this is one area where software has not yet permeated. And when software touches something, it takes off."* [10] Because the technology is still in a very early stage, though, it is likely to take off in directions that are impossible to predict. If I were to make bets, I'd bet on 3D printing influencing the way space colonists dine in the future. But, just like there is more to eating than simply growing vegetables, there's more to living than eating. So, aside from dining, what might it actually be like to live on Titan?

As we discussed earlier, two of the biggest differences between Titan and Earth are the cold temperatures and the lack of oxygen in the atmosphere. However, the air pressure is comparable to Earth. In fact, according to McKay, *"If you lived on Titan, you wouldn't need a pressurized suit to survive; all you'd really need is an oxygen mask and very warm clothing."* The good news is, both of these technologies exist, and with little modification could be used to survive on Titan.

Part of what makes Titan such an exciting place is its thick atmosphere, which would protect inhabitants from harmful radiation. *"In terms of pressure, standing on the surface would feel similar to resting at the bottom of a pool on Earth."* McKay explains. The other different feeling would be the difference of gravity on Titan – its gravity is just 14% of that on Earth, which is actually less than the gravity on our own moon. *"But because of Titan's low*

10 Evarts, Holly. 2016. "Dinner In 3D". *The Fu Foundation School Of Engineering & Applied Science - Columbia University.* http://engineering.columbia.edu/news/hod-lipson-3d-food-printing.

gravity and dense atmosphere, you could jump off a high spot and use your coat to glide down." McKay joked, *"Hang gliding would take on a whole new meaning."*[11]

Unfortunately, there is more to living on Titan than gliding off of cliffs with an oxygen tank. Remember, Titan is *cold* . . . very, very cold. And although Titan is much different from Earth, we do have a place on our planet that is close(ish) to the harsh, infinite winter of Titan: Antarctica. If we want to know where to start, we can look at the habitats in Antarctica for inspiration.

Halley VI Antarctic Research Station

In 2012, the British Antarctic Society opened the world's first fully transportable polar research station, Halley VI. The habitat is stationed on the 130-meter-thick Brunt Ice Shelf, which is located on the northern coast of Antarctica. The shelf flows slowly out into the Weddell Sea, and breaks off into chunks, forming icebergs. This means that the station has to be transportable, otherwise it would eventually break into the sea.

To solve this problem, the entire station is built using modules on hydraulic skis, which can be lifted to raise the station above the snow. This also allows the 8 modules to be separated and pulled with bulldozers to a new location. The station was designed to have the least environmental impact on the ice as possible.

Halley VI accommodates approximately 70 staff during the Antarctic summer, and 16 "winterers" (staff who stay over the winter). Researchers conduct experiments to study global issues, ranging from climate change to sea level rise, space weather, and the ozone hole.

---

11 Castro, Joseph. 2015. "What It Would Be Like To Live On Saturn's Moons Titan And Enceladus". *Space.Com.* https://www.space.com/28786-living-on-saturn-moons-titan-enceladus.html.

But it gets cold. And lonely. And when it is completely dark 105 days out of the year, morale can deteriorate rapidly. So how do the researchers deal with these conditions?

When the station was designed, there was a focus on creating architecture that improved the living conditions of the researchers staying inside. The British Antarctic Society hired and worked with a color psychologist to create a custom color palette to help offset the effects of living in total darkness. Designers created special alarm clocks to create artificial sunlight, helping the researchers maintain more consistent biorhythms.

To help with the feeling of deprivation from nature, special scented wood veneers were used to create a sense of the outdoors. This also helps researchers cope with the lack of greenery. Lighting designers were consulted to create simulations of daylight, which help make the researches feel more at home. The interior was designed to offer isolated spaces, as well as group spaces— this helps people with social interaction and the issues of working and living in isolation.[12]

If we think about the way stations in Antarctica are designed, we can apply many of the same principles to the way we could design and build stations for Titan. What would need to be modified in order for them to work on Titan?

Oxygen, which we've covered, is obviously the big one. But the weather is really the second-largest issue, because, while Titan is much, much colder than Antarctica, the weather is also slightly more unruly. While dry periods may last for decades, bases on Titan must be prepared for flooding and torrential downpours. Habitats would likely need to be designed, like Halley, to be moved

12 Broughton, Hugh. 2013. "Behind The Architecture Of The UK's Antarctic Station". *British Council*. https://www.britishcouncil.org/voices-magazine/behind-the-architecture-of-the-uks-antarctic-station.

around. They could even be designed to float, in the event of flooding.

When it comes to scale, stations on Titan would need to be much larger than those in Antarctica. Even the largest bases in the summer only host about 1,000 people, and none of these people live there full time. In order to have a self-sustainable colony on Titan, we would need to send much larger groups of people.

I talked with Sarah Johnson, an incredible planetary scientist who has actually lived and researched in Antarctica (though not at the Halley station). *"So, what's it like living there?"* I asked. Sarah laughed as she replied, *"You know, it's cold."* Though it's cold, Sarah says that the view is worth it. *"I mean, it's so absolutely, stunningly beautiful. I feel like I can't get enough of spending time in the dry valleys."* While it is beautiful, Sarah explained the main difference— communication.

"It does feel very far from everything, everything that is going on back home in the States. There are very few people out there. I think the biggest thing I noticed was there you can't use a cell phone, there's some wireless connectivity but it's incredibly limited, it takes hours to send an email," Sarah explained. *"It's just a big difference to go from here [in the States] where everybody's on their phone all the time and just totally connected to what's happening in the world."*

WHAT WOULD IT ACTUALLY BE LIKE TO LIVE ON TITAN?

Saturn. . . That is, I believe, the first word that would pop into anyone's head for the first few days (or maybe even months) each morning as he or she awakens. The image of Saturn would be a huge fixture in the sky for those who live on Titan. Imagine waking up, opening your curtains, and looking out across the light, orange sky, the ringed planet looming over the horizon— if you were a colonist on Titan, this would be your view. The size of Saturn on the horizon would appear eleven times larger than the moon appears on Earth.

Wait. . . An *orange* sky? Why would the sky be orange?

If you're familiar with "atmospheric reddening," then you know that our sky is blue during the day because the other color of the light from the sun (red) bounces off of our atmosphere, and only the blue light shines through (personally, I think we should call it "atmospheric blueing," but no one asked me). On Titan, the compounds in Titan's thick atmosphere reflect more blue light than red, giving those on the surface an orange sky. Sunrises and sunsets would appear blue, in a sort of opposite from Earth's (this is a rather simplistic explanation, so to any physicists reading this: please don't get mad!).

What about the Sun?

The Sun would be visible to colonists on Titan as a small, bright spot, one tenth of the size that we see from Earth. This means that looking out even in broad daylight would feel dim, and even a sunny, clear sky would feel like an overcast evening on Earth. The *Huygens* probe found the brightness of the surface of Titan to be about one thousand times dimmer than full solar illumination on Earth (that's the same thing as the light levels we experience about ten minutes after sunset on Earth).

And the landscape?

The landscape on Titan features rocky deserts, sandy dunes, and lakes of methane. Taking a walk on Titan might resemble walking through Yellowstone National Park here on Earth.

The seasons, on the other hand, can only really be compared to fantasy worlds. Think *Game of Thrones*, with the seasons lasting 7 years each. The weather is likely much more stable than that on Earth, but its mood swings are wide: they may feature torrential downpours of methane, causing flash floods, which would then subside and lead to decades or even centuries of drought.

Oh, right . . . *rain*.

Titan is the only other place in the solar system that we know to have hydrological cycle (the equivalent of the water cycle on Earth, but made of methane). Titan not only has rivers, lakes and seas of methane, but rain as well.

Did I just say lakes, rivers, and even seas of methane? Sounds like a business opportunity. . . .

Why wouldn't we mine Titan for its resources, like we would on the moon?

When people think about going to other planets, one of the first opportunities that comes to mind is the collection of resources. Historically, economic opportunity has driven expansion to new territories— the first mass expansion westward in the United States only came after the discovery of gold. The Gold Rush led to some 300,000 people moving from all over the world to California in the mid 1800's, in an attempt to start over and get rich. A similar mentality is often associated with the potential for colonizing other planets— in science fiction movies, this is often the case. In James Cameron's *Avatar,* the entire reason humans have come to the planet is to gather a rare mineral, "unobtanium," for profit. The humans destroy the native habitat in an attempt to make money and bring the resource back to earth.

In reality, though, the idea of shipping resources over far distances, such as from Titan or even just Mars (which is much, much closer to us), is extremely impractical. Even when the atmosphere of Titan actually rains natural gas, it doesn't make sense to go there with the intention of shipping it back to earth. Experts like Elon Musk tell us that the cost of shipping these goods back is too high to be economically viable, and the resources on these planets would be much better used to colonize those other planets.

"Any natural resource extraction on Mars, the output would be for Mars, it definitely wouldn't make sense to transport stuff 200 million miles back to Earth," Musk said in an interview at MIT in 2014. *"If*

you had crack cocaine on Mars, like in pre-packaged pallets, it still wouldn't make sense to bring it back here. It may mean good times for the Martians, but not back here," he joked.[13]

The bottom line is, the resources on other planets are best suited to be used for colonization of that planet. While Musk is focused on Mars, the same principle applies to Titan, or any other place we end up going. While things could certainly change far in the future, for now, the reason to go to Titan remains to be for the establishment of a colony and the preservation of humanity.

And when it comes to humanity, the key is to actually maintain a stable (and eventually growing) population of humans. And while there are a lot of issues that arise when we think practically about taking a colony to another planet or moon, one of the important is one that we have yet to solve: How will humans reproduce in low gravity?

The three main issues with human reproduction in Space:

- Gravity
- Radiation
- Genetic Variation

The Problem of Gravity:

Children born on Titan would likely never be able to return to Earth. Their bones and muscles would be conditioned to Titan's lower gravity, and Earth's forces would feel crushing to them.

---

13 Smith, Marcia. 2014. "Elon Musk: Lipstick Or A Colony On Mars?". *Space Policy Online*. https://spacepolicyonline.com/news/elon-musk-lipstick-or-a-colony-on-mars/.

Unfortunately, there isn't much research currently being done to solve this issue, but it will be a major one that will have to be addressed in order to maintain a self-sustaining colony on Titan.

The Problem of Radiation:

"The present shielding capabilities would probably preclude having a pregnancy transited to Mars," radiation biophysicist Tore Straume of NASA Ames Research Center told Space.com.

Studies in primates have shown that even small doses of radiation can kill most immature egg cells in female fetuses. This means that females conceived in space, and exposed to higher levels of radiation, would likely be born sterile due to damage to eggs.

"One would have to be very protective of those cells during gestation, during pregnancy, to make sure that the female didn't become sterile so they could continue the colony," Straume said.

Luckily, due to Titan's thick atmosphere, once the colonists arrived on the moon, they'd be safe from harmful radiation. Colonists making the journey to the moon would likely have to rely on contraceptive measures to prevent pregnancy during the journey.

"This is an issue that really needs to be resolved if we ever plan to have a colony on Mars," or anywhere else, for that matter, Straume concluded.[14]

Genetic Variation:

When humans reproduce in small, isolated populations even here on Earth, inbreeding causes genetic mutations that are harmful. For example, European royalty suffered a myriad of health issues

---

14 Minkel, JR. 2011. "Sex And Pregnancy On Mars: A Risky Proposition". *Space. Com.* https://www.space.com/10822-sex-mars-pregnancy-space-risks.html.

due to generations of inbreeding. When colonizing space, we would need to make sure that we send large enough numbers of people in order to keep the population stocked with genetic diversity.[15] According to Portland State University anthropologist, Cameron Smith, the ideal number of colonists needed to maintain near 100 percent genetic diversity is between 10,000 and 40,000.[16] While these numbers could be padded by sending frozen embryos, the bottom line is that more research will need to be done before we're ready to raise the first Titanian children.

No matter how we look at it, colonizing Titan today would be completely impossible. . . but we *are* well on our way. Between printed food and wing suits, we are, one by one, solving the issues and questions that need to be addressed before we can colonize Saturn's moon. Could it happen in my lifetime? If we continue dreaming, planning, and researching, the answer is yes. I already have my umbrella packed. You know, for the rain.

15 Gorvett, Zaria. 2016. "Could Just Two People Repopulate Earth?". *BBC*. http://www.bbc.com/future/story/20160113-could-just-two-people-repopulate-earth.
16 Fessenden, Marissa. 2015. "Houston, We Might Have Some Major Problems Making Babies In Space". *Smithsonian*. https://www.smithsonianmag.com/smart-news/houston-we-might-have-some-major-problems-making-babies-space-180954828/.

CHAPTER 6

SPACE STATION

___

"It is often difficult for a person who is not familiar with current exploration projects and technological advances to distinguish between science fiction because we can't do it, or science fiction because we have not done it yet." - Bryan Versteeg wrote in 2015[1]

Ever seen the movie *Interstellar*?

The movie, directed by Christopher Nolan, is set in a future where the earth is dying, slowly becoming uninhabitable due to dust storms. The plot focuses on the journey of Joseph Cooper, a former NASA pilot who has been focusing on raising his two children and farming corn since the shutdown of the space program. When Cooper is recruited to return to NASA, he's sent on a mission to find a new, habitable world for humans to colonize. While the movie is fictional, many of the plot's important points are based on real space science. In fact, they even made some new discoveries *about* space while preparing for the film.[2]

___

1 Versteeg, Bryan. 2015. "Kalpana One". *Medium*. https://medium.com/space-anthropology/kalpana-one-318f4e3bef40.
2 Warner Brothers. 2014. *Interstellar – Building A Black Hole*. Video. https://www.youtube.com/watch?v=MfGfZwQ_qaY.

One of the plot points of the movie centers around a black hole, which, to put it simply, is the remnants of a collapsed star in which gravity is so dense that it actually bends space-time and sucks light in from the universe. The actual physics behind black holes is incredibly complicated, and the equations to predict the way light behaves can take up pages and pages of notes. When Christopher Nolan decided he wanted to show the black hole on screen, he contacted Kip Thorne, a world renowned astrophysicist and Nobel laureate known for his work in gravitational physics. Nolan introduced Thorne and Paul Franklin, a senior supervisor at the Academy-Awards-winning Double Negative effects house.

The two worked with a talented team of artists to render a realistic black hole — no easy task, and one that had never before been attempted. *"It's very easy to fall into the trap of breaking the rules of reality,"* says Franklin, *"and those rules are actually quite strict."* While computer graphics artists have techniques for rendering light and reflections in films, those tools operate on the assumption that light is traveling on straight paths — paths that are not followed by the light around black holes.

The team at Double Negative worked to create a completely new rendering software using the equations from Thorne, computing the complex paths of light caused by the black hole— a task that led individual frames to take up to 100 hours to render, and used nearly 800 terabytes of data. In the end, the results were well worth the wait. *"Science fiction always wants to dress things up, like it's never happy with the ordinary universe,"* Franklin says. *"What we were getting out of the software was compelling, straight-off."* Beyond creating a breathtaking scene for the film, their work led to Thorne's publication of two different scientific papers — one for the physics community, and the other for the computer graphics community.[3]

One important takeaway from this — science fiction can inspire real science. But the reverse is also true: in the end of the film, we see Cooper Station, the massive space colony in orbit around Saturn. While *Interstellar's* Cooper Station is fictional, the design was largely based on existing proposals for space stations. One of the main plot points of *Interstellar* was the necessity of solving the equation that would help NASA counteract gravity, in order to launch the massive station from Earth. In reality, we wouldn't need to do this— space stations can be built in space.

Even the International Space Station was built in parts, with the first modules sent up in 1998. The station now covers an area as big as a football field, and weighs almost 400 tons (we don't have rockets powerful enough to send this much directly to space even if we wanted to). The station was launched in pieces, and took over 40 missions to construct — in fact, modules are still being planned to this day.[4]

While taking humans to other planets will require research and the development of technology that is not currently available, space stations built in space could be the answer. With enough money and new applications of current technology, these stations are possible. Some of these concepts are older than space travel itself, in fact, yet their planning has been so meticulously thought-out, that the designs and logistics of them have remained virtually unchanged – in some cases – after almost a century.

---

3 Rogers, Adam. 2015. "How Building A Black Hole For Interstellar Led To An Amazing Scientific Discovery". *WIRED.* https://www.wired.com/2014/10/astrophysics-interstellar-black-hole/.

4 "Building The International Space Station". 2018. *European Space Agency.* http://www.esa.int/Our_Activities/Human_Spaceflight/International_Space_Station/Building_the_International_Space_Station3.

HERMAN POTOČNIK'S *WOHNRAD* (LIVING WHEEL):

There has been a long history of humans looking for a home among the stars, beginning even before anyone had set foot on the moon. Beginning even before we had ever launched anything into orbit. For example, in 1928, Herman Potočnik published the book, *The Problem of Space Travel*, in which he discussed his ideas for a spacefaring future of humanity. The 188-page book featured 100 hand-drawn illustrations and outlined the establishment of a permanent human space settlement.

The book, as far as we know, is the first published plan of architecture in space. It laid out the details of a Wohnrad, or "Living Wheel," that would rotate as it sat in space. The centrifugal force of the rotation would be used to generate artificial gravity. Imagine a massive doughnut-shaped station, spinning slowly in space.

The station itself would be a 100-foot ring-shaped structure. It would use a large parabolic mirror system to focus sunlight, which, in turn, would heat water pipes, steam-powering the station. The proposed purpose was for a detailed observation of the ground (for both peaceful and military use). He described how the station could be used to conduct useful scientific research, and weighed doubts about the potentially destructive power of these discoveries for military use. Does any of this sound familiar?

While Potočnik was unknown at the time of his death – he died at the age of 36, in poverty, his work completely unnoticed – he received quite a high compliment when his proposal was used as the inspiration for Space Station V in Stanley Kubrick's *2001: A Space Odyssey*. In fact, Kubrik's use of Potočnik's designs, gave the engineer far more recognition than he had ever received while alive.

BERNAL SPHERE - "ISLAND ONE":

In 1929, J.D Bernal, a popular Irish scientist, proposed the idea of a spherical space station. Spheres are the optimal shape for any space station, as they have the greatest mass efficiency for radiation shielding, and also optimize the amount of necessary oxygen. Why spheres? With a little bit of math you can prove this yourself, so I won't drag it out (remember—I'm not a huge math fan), but the shape of a sphere has the lowest possible surface area to volume ratio. If you don't trust me, Neil DeGrasse Tyson explained it well in 1997:

"It can be shown using freshman-level calculus that the one and only shape that has the smallest surface area for an enclosed volume is a perfect sphere. In fact, billions of dollars could be saved annually on packaging materials if all shipping boxes and all packages of food in the supermarket were spheres. For example, the contents of a super-jumbo box of Cheerios would fit easily into a spherical carton that had a four-and-a-half inch radius. But practical matters prevail—nobody wants to chase food down the aisle after it rolls off the shelves."[5]

What does that mean for a space station? A spherical space station would have less surface area for more interior volume than any other shaped station. That's good for us because it means less surface area to shield from radiation. Bernal's design would allow for the greatest amount of interior space for a given size. Again, just like the *Wohnrad*, this was proposed at a time when no one had yet sent anything to orbit, and it would be another forty years before anyone thought seriously of Bernal's proposal.

Then hit space station craze of the 1970's. Humans had just stepped foot on the moon, funding for NASA was ample, and the minds of

---

5 DeGrasse Tyson, Neil. 1997. "On Being Round". *Hayden Planetarium*. http://www.haydenplanetarium.org/tyson/read/1997/03/01/on-being-round.

many were focused on the potential futures for humanity. In 1975, Gerard K. O'Neill refined Bernal's original idea, and proposed a new version of the Bernal Sphere, known as "Island One."

The sphere would have a diameter of only 500m, and would rotate at 1.9 RPM, producing artificial gravity. The interior landscape would resemble a large valley running along the equator of the sphere, with a "Crystal Palace" habitat used for agriculture. Large mirrors would provide sunlight, and the whole thing would create a livable habitat for 10,000 people.

O'Neill later proposed an "Island Two," meant to be a larger version of the Island One, with an 1800m diameter (4 mile circumference at the equator). The size of this habitat was optimized for economics — the habitat had to be large enough to support an efficient industrial base, but small enough to allow for efficient transportation within the habitat.

THE O'NEILL CYLINDER - "ISLAND THREE":

O'Neill didn't just build off of others' proposed space station ideas; he had some very important ideas of his own. In 1974 he published an article in *Physics Today* that mentioned his own type of space station— the O'Neill Cylinder. Later, in 1976, he published his book, *The High Frontier: Human Colonies in Space,* where he fully fleshed out his idea.

The O'Neill Cylinder would feature two 20-mile long cylinders connected by a rod and bearing systems on each end. They would be rotating in opposite directions in order to keep the station aimed towards the sun (rotating in the same direction would introduce a gyroscopic torque, ,which could, in turn, introduce a terrifying and uncontrollable wobble). Each of the cylinders would be 5 miles in diameter, rotating at a set speed of twenty-eight rotations per hour. This rotation will provide artificial gravity to inhabitants. The outer layer would be a 10 mile radius agricultural ring, rotating at a slightly different speed to support farming. Between the two cylinders, there would be an industrial manufacturing space, with minimized gravity allowing for speedier manufacturing processes. Overall, the station would contain 500 square miles of living space and could support several million people.[6]

How does Artificial Gravity work?

Earth's gravitational force comes from its mass, which is the only known natural source of gravity. Though the exact workings of gravity are still debated, the known constants regarding gravity are that two masses are attracted to each other by a force – a force we call "gravity." There's more to it than that, of course (mass and size of the object, momentum of one or more of the objects, resistance to movement, etc.), but we stick to the earth because the earth has a very, very large mass. In space, of course, we would not be close enough to the Earth (or other planets) for gravity to have a sufficient pull on us. How, then, do we create gravity?

Have you ever ridden a ride at a carnival where you stand in a cylinder, back to the wall, and begin to spin? It's probably called something like "The Gravitron" or "The Rotor," and likely smells ever-so-slightly of someone's lost lunch. Eventually the floor drops away and you're left pressed back to the wall "floating" above the floor. This carnival ride uses the principle of centrifugal force. So do proposed space stations.

Artificial gravity is a fancy name for the use of centrifugal force, in which the station spins, creating a force that acts to pull the inhabitants to the outside of the station. Depending on the scale of the station and the rotation rate, different levels of "gravity" can be simulated. The reason carnival goers might feel sick on the ride

---

6 O'Neill, Gerard K. 1974. "The Colonization Of Space – Gerard K. O'Neill, Physics Today, 1974". *National Space Society*. http://space.nss.org/the-colonization-of-space-gerard-k-o-neill-physics-today-1974/.

is due to the excess g forces created, sometimes upwards of 2 to 3 times Earth's gravity (a ride that simulated the feeling of just lying on the floor wouldn't be nearly as fun). On a space station, the rotation speed would be specifically designed to create Earth-like gravitational forces.

"When you stand on the ground on the earth, which way is the force of gravity? Down. So why don't you fall in a straight line to the center of the Earth? Because the surface of the earth pushes up on your shoes with the exact same force but in the opposite direction! Same idea in the space station: the centrifugal "force" appears to push objects outward, but the strength of the space station provides an opposing "centripetal force" which pushes inward. The end result is that it feels similar to walking on the surface of a planet (if the space station is spinning at the right speed)."— Ryan Anderson, a research fellow at USGS in Flagstaff, AZ[7]

Each of the human habitats on Island Three would rotate twenty-eight times per hour. This would minimize the effects of motion sickness, so that only a few sensitive people would even notice. A person standing still in the station would be able to detect the spin-ward and anti-spin-ward directions by turning his or her head, but otherwise feel just like they would on Earth. Standing on the "ground" of the station would only be slightly different – from a gravitational standpoint – than standing on the real ground of Earth.

Another difference is that objects dropped in space would fall in curves instead of straight lines. This can cause confusion for flying species, such as bees and birds, and would make playing a sport like soccer confusing for colonists who learned to play on Earth

---

7 Anderson, Ryan. 2006. "Can Artificial Gravity Be Created In Space?". *Ask An Astronomer*. http://curious.astro.cornell.edu/150-people-in-astronomy/space-exploration-and-astronauts/general-questions/927-can-artificial-gravity-be-created-in-space-intermediate.

(for those who are interested, this phenomenon is a product of something called a Coriolis force. We have it here on Earth, too, it's just so slight and so prevalent that no one notices). Of course, there's more to life than walking and gravity . . . . well, okay, so gravity is a pretty big deal. Still, there's more to living on a space station than gravity, so how would our actual way of life feel on a space station?

Each cylinder would have six equal sections, three transparent windows and three strips of land. A person standing on a strip of land would be able to look up and out a large window. The windows of the station would be paired with large, hinged mirrors pointed towards the sun. As the "day" progresses, the mirrors would slowly move, creating a natural progression of sun angles. Night would be produced by fully opening the mirrors and allowing the window to view open space. A person living in the station would be able to experience a normal 24-hour day, just as a person on Earth would.

Life on a space station would be quite similar to life in a small town on Earth. Each station could be designed with different amenities, such as parks or sports complexes. When it comes to thinking about a person's daily life on space stations, it seems like such a far-off topic that it can be hard to imagine. As man has come closer and closer to building space habitats, these designs have gone through a few refinement processes. Kalpana-1, for example, utilizes the O'Neill Cylinder idea, but has been given a more *artistic* design than some of the other stations.

The station, designed by Al Globus, Nitin Arora, Ankur Bajoria, and Joe Strout, incorporates both the technical aspects (vital to a proposal), and the design work of Bryan Versteeg. What is magical about Bryan's work is that he designs every inch of the station, down to golf courses, lakes, even forests, and I had the chance to talk with him about his process. As an artist who loves space, this was really exciting to me (I had a fangirl moment for sure when I got his reply that he'd be willing to talk).

"If you were to say we have a settlement that has a radius of 250 meters that has a length of 300 meters, and a population of 2,200, or 12,000 people, the numbers are in your mind— but you still don't really get a sense of the volume and the spaciousness and of the community." Bryan explained. While those numbers might sound technically impressive, can you really imagine living there?

Now what if I showed you a picture, a beautiful lush green park, a group of people walking up slightly curved fields? Next I show an image of a beautiful home, with a back porch, four cozy lawn chairs round a table, greenery unfolding in the background. These are the kind of images Bryan produces, and it seems a lot more appealing, right? "Once you see it, it really changes everything. It changes your understanding of the space." Bryan said, "I flesh out those numbers with people in space and trees and structure so that so that you can actually, you know, get an idea of what it would look like."

Beyond what it would look like, Bryan takes into consideration what it would *feel* like to live in the places he's designing. "I've always been really interested in the human element of architecture and the interface between people and their built environment. I want to get into these places from eye level," he told me. "I like being able to put things that seem very familiar to us into this very unfamiliar environment."

We talked about the importance of community in space stations. Many of Bryan's designs center around a communal space. "The square itself is kind of the gathering point for the whole community," he explains. When it comes to space stations, "essentially you want these walkable communities that have been successful in design for thousands of years, and still have that value today."

Can it Happen?

Remember when we talked about the moon becoming a sort of industrial base, used for mining its resources? When it comes to creating space stations, the moon could be a very useful stepping stone. O'Neill knew that these stations would be too expensive to build by launching materials from Earth. Many of the materials needed, he theorized, could be manufactured and shipped from the Moon. He proposed the idea of using an electromagnetic mass driver to launch lunar materials into space. Basically, rather than using a rocket to launch materials from the Moon, the mass driver would essentially *push* the construction materials so fast that they would fly off of the Moon and out into space.[8]

While there are obvious problems to overcome – construction is just one of the examples – many of those problems have been, and are being, investigated and worked out even now. Engineers are, for example, very close to closing the oxygen *and* water loops, allowing the stations to become more self-sustaining. While mining resources from asteroids and other planets is not fully feasible yet, once it is, then placing a station near a resource-rich planet or moon would allow us to then reach further into space, building newer stations. It would be like using giant, cosmic stepping stones to cross a river.

But what do we do once we have that first stone? We keep stepping. And keep stepping. And keep stepping, until we can colonize a planet. And then another. And then another.

----

8 David, Leonard. 2017. "Could Moon Miners Use Railguns To Launch Ore Into Space?". *Space.Com*. https://www.space.com/36442-could-moon-miners-use-railguns-to-launch-ore-into-space.html.

"We've always defined ourselves by the ability to overcome the impossible. And we count these moments. These moments when we dare to aim higher, to break barriers, to reach for the stars, to make the unknown known. We count these moments as our proudest achievements. But we lost all that. Or perhaps we've just forgotten that we are still pioneers. And we've barely begun. And that our greatest accomplishments cannot be behind us, because our destiny lies above us."

- Joseph Cooper in *Interstellar*

CHAPTER 7

WHAT'S NEXT?

"Imagination will often carry us to worlds that never were. But without it we go nowhere" – Carl Sagan

After creating colonies on Titan (or creating rotating doughnuts and death-star-like stations), where else might we go?

Some of Saturn's other moons, such as Enceladus, or Jupiter's Europa, are interesting potentials. Enceladus actively spouts water into space from its icy surface. Unfortunately, while the presence of liquid water means Enceladus might have the potential to harbor alien life, that doesn't necessarily make it the ideal candidate to support human life. Its gravity is only 1% of Earth's, and a radius of only 252 km (giving it a surface area roughly the size of Texas).

Europa, on the other hand, has a significantly larger gravity than Enceldaus (although it is still only 13% of Earth's gravity), and has a radius of 1,561 km. I'd take Europa as the next place in our solar system to send human explorers. Once we've solved the issues of getting to and colonizing Titan— heading to Europa next makes logical sense.

Creating a colony on Europa is not without its own unique challenges. While temperatures at the equator never rise above -260F, and the gravity on Europa is just 13% of that on Earth, this would be nothing new to the Titan colonists. The difference? The surface of Europa is one massive ice block, literally — solid water ice. European colonists (what else would you call them?) might enjoy a day off ice skating along the surface — imagine the tricks you could do with that gravity! Too bad, though, that you'd have to skate in a clunky space suit.

Just like our moon here on Earth, Europa does not have an atmosphere, so anything living on the surface would be bombarded with cosmic radiation (and as we've discussed, that's not so good for living things). So we can't live on the surface of Europa, either. Unfortunately, unlike our moon, there's no abundance of regolith with which to coat our habitats. Seems dire, right?

Not to worry! Europa's icy surface is just a thick crust above a massive liquid water ocean. Tunneling into the ice and creating habitats below the surface would provide the protection radiation, as well as access to the water needed to produce oxygen and survive.

Scientists on Earth are already living in underwater habitats for months at a time. Ian Koblick, an underwater explorer and aquanaut, opened the La Chalupa underwater research facility/ habitat in 1972. At the time, this was the largest and most advanced facility of its kind in the world. Since then, even though popular interest in sending humans underwater has faded, advancements continue to be made. When it comes to building self-sustaining underwater colonies here on earth, Koblick tells us that it is entirely possible. *"There are no technological hurdles,"* he says. *"If you had the money and the need, you could do it today."*[1]

---

1 Nuwer, Rachel. 2013. "Will We Ever... Live In Underwater Cities?". *BBC*. http:// www.bbc.com/future/story/20130930-can-we-build-underwater-cities.

While doing this in space obviously presents greater technical challenges, the same principle applies — with the right people, enough money, and the pure desire to succeed, habitats on places like Europa are possible. Especially if we've already colonized Titan and created settlements on our own moon, many of the challenges facing the settlers of Europa will have already been solved. Though some of the technology still might not yet exist, there is little doubt that it will be possible.

When we think about civilizations today, most people would consider the human race to be fairly advanced. There's even an old saying in which a man walks into a patent office and asks, *"Where might I speak to a patent officer?"* A young boy replies, *"There are no officers, Sir. Everything that can be invented has been invented."* This reflects the attitude of many people in society today who think that life on earth is pretty much as good as it's going to get. The truth is that we're quite far from inventing everything, and even further from being considered an advanced society when compared with our potential.

In 1964, Russian physicist Nikolai Kardashev came up with a scale to rank civilizations' levels of technological and cultural advancement. He believed that the status of a culture depends on two things: energy, and technology. His theory posits that a civilization's level of technological advancement is dependent on their use of energy— in other words, the more energy a society can produce, the more advanced it is.

Kardashev theorized that the development of technology would enable civilizations to harness energy, which would lead to more enlightened social systems and, in turn, lead to a thriving culture. He developed The Kardashev Scale, which he used to "measure" this advancement. The scale originally included three categories: Types I, II, and III, and also included a Type 0, for civilizations below the lowest threshold.

The types of civilizations include:

Type 0: *Subglobal Culture*. This is a civilization confined to its home planet. It would be reliant on energy from crude organic materials (wood, coal, oil). This basically means that everything this civilization uses is from its home planet, but they have not yet even harnessed the full energy of their home planet. Humans living in 2018 are an example of a Type 0 civilization.

Type I: *Planetary Culture*. This is a civilization that is able to harness all the energy from its home planet (for us on Earth that would be around 10^{15} watts). Living in this type of civilization would mean having complete control over the planet, including weather systems, volcanic eruptions, even influencing the geological makeup of the planet. Members of this civilization would harness the power of their entire planet, and would soon begin to populate other planets in their solar system. Scientists believe that humans on Earth have the potential to reach a Type 1 civilization in as soon as 100 years, so long as technological advancement maintains its current rate.

Type II: *Stellar Culture*. This is a civilization that is able to harness all the energy of its star (for us orbiting the sun, that would be 10^{26} watts), as well as the mining of asteroids, as well as the colonization of many other planets/moons in the solar system. There have been methods proposed for harnessing the energy of the sun, such as the Dyson Sphere (a giant sphere that harnesses the power of a star— often seen in science fiction). This civilization would control everything from the orbits of all planets in the system to the paths of asteroids and comets. This is like the Federation of Planets in *Star Trek*. Probably not us for another 1000 years, or so. Once we are able to colonize Titan and Europa, we'll be on track to becoming a Type II civilization.

Type III: *Galactic Culture*. This civilization would harness the output of a galaxy— controlling the energy from *all* of the stars in that galaxy. This civilization would be capable of moving planets across star systems, merging solar systems and stars, and even creating stars. Citizens would have colonized star systems across the galaxy, populated countless planets/worlds, and be capable of highly-efficient interstellar travel. They would have likely developed some way to warp space in order to travel efficiently (like Hyperspace in *Star Wars*, or the wormhole in *Interstellar*). This civilization would be able to harness 10 billion times the energy output of a Type II civilization. An example of this would be the Empire in *Star Wars*.

This is where Kardashev himself left off. He believed that anything beyond a Type III was not likely possible, so he didn't entertain anything further. Other scientists have picked up where he left off, though, and proposed a Type IV, V, and even a Type VI Culture.

Type IV: *Universal Culture.* This would be an intergalactic culture, capable of harnessing the power of multiple, or even all, galaxies (a billion, trillion suns). Members of this civilization have probably achieved some sort of immortality. Some believe that they might even live in utopian societies inside of black holes. An example of this would be a Time Lord (like The Doctor) on BBC's *Doctor Who*.

Type V: *Multiverse Culture.* Members of this civilization have transcended their universe. With the rising popularity of string theory, this civilization type has become more accepted as a possibility. Citizens would be able to jump between multiverses that contain varied forms of matter, physics, and space-time. The Ancient One from *Doctor Strange* could be a sci-fi example of this.

Though this is where the mainstream definition of the scale ends, some scientists have gone sp far as to propose a Type VI. This civilization would go beyond the multiverse, transcending space time itself. Members would be able to create and destroy entire universes and multiverses. The idea of a God or Deity would fit in to the Type VI civilization.

While we are not even on the scale yet, we have the potential to become a Type I society within the 21st century. I am certain that it is completely possible for humanity to reach a Type II society within the millennia if we expand our exploration into space now. We don't need to have another 5000 year gap between leveling up. Now, you might be thinking that this is all a little too theoretical — after all, how can we compare ourselves to things that don't even exist? How do we judge ourselves on a scale that was, quite literally, made up? Well, that's just where the fun begins, and where science-fiction meets reality, because, after we establish colonies within our own solar system, the next reasonable goal, as outlined by Kardashev, is to continue on and colonize another star system.

When I asked Damian Balla, the lead manufacturing engineer at the University of Southern California's Rocket Propulsion Lab, about the potential for humans to travel to another star system, Alpha Centauri — the closest star system to the Sun — was his first choice.

Alpha Centauri A and B are two stars that form the the binary star system known as Alpha Centauri AB (a much smaller third star, known as Proxima Centauri, is loosely orbiting the two). They're about the same distance from each other as our sun is to Uranus and orbit a common center of gravity every 80 years. Have you ever wished to see a binary sunset like the iconic scene right before Luke leaves his home on Tatooine in the original *Star Wars*?

Well, to beings living on a planet in this star system, every sunset would look something like that. While Damian warned me, *"[the discussion will] have to be slightly more theoretical just because we have no feasible means of doing it right now,"* I couldn't help but get excited about the possibilities of having my own Luke Skywalker moment. *"But that being said,"* Damian continued, *"it probably could use a lot of the technologies that we will have to develop for deep space missions."* So, exactly, what would we need to do to get there?

Alpha Centauri is 4.367 light years away, and while Damian believes it's possible for us to make the journey, *"Propulsion . . . would have to fundamentally change,"* he told me. With our current propulsion methods, it would take us somewhere around 50,000 years to arrive.[2]

Again, not good.

Damian believes that with time, we will be able to figure out a way to travel faster. And if we're to do that, *"20% the speed of light would get us there in about 20 years, which is ridiculous, but it would be awesome."*

Scientists have long been trying to solve the issues of propulsion.

The concept of a radio frequency resonant cavity thruster, popularly known as an Em Drive, was first hypothesized when Roger Shawyer published the concept in 2001. What's so interesting about the concept is that it generates thrust by bouncing microwaves around inside a cone-shaped chamber. There's no fuel burned, nor exhaust produced -- the drive defies the laws of Newtonian physics.

In 2016, there was quite the buzz around the internet when scientists at NASA tested the theory and actually produced some thrust. Though they haven't ruled out the possibility of errors or determined exactly why this occurred (what's so weird about the technology is that none of the tests have been repeatable), we may see physics-defying propulsion methods in the future. However, even if we do not, we *will* figure out a way to get to another star system somehow.[3]

2 "#5: Stephen Hawking's Warning: Abandon Earth—Or Face Extinction". 2017. *Big Think.* http://bigthink.com/dangerous-ideas/5-stephen-hawkings-warning-abandon-earth-or-face-extinction.

3 Wall, Mike. 2016. "Test Of 'Impossible' Emdrive Space Engine Passes Peer Review". *Space.Com.* https://www.space.com/34797-impossible-space-engine-emdrive-study-published.html.

Another theory on how we could potentially get to other stars would be to travel in a modified version of the space stations discussed in the last chapter – or something like the *Axiom* from Disney Pixar's *Wall-E* (remember the massive cruise-ship city in space, where all the people adapted to living in chairs?) Though this is going into the realm of science fiction, there's definitely a possibility that future colonists will arrive at other star systems in a similar way.

What other sci-fi-esque theoretical concepts are scientists working on?

Asteroid mining. Remember when we talked about getting resources from the moon and using them to build habitats and space stations? Some companies believe that we could catch and mine asteroids for similar purposes. Companies, such as Deep Space Industries, whose website explains:

> *Asteroid resources include all the same materials planets are made of, providing an abundant supply of exactly what we need in space. Specifically, C-group and related classes of asteroids contain high abundances of water and important elements — including organic carbon, sulfur, nitrogen, and phosphorus — as well as ferrous metals.*

> *The initial targets for mining are those that pass through Earth's neighborhood. Many water-rich Near Earth Asteroids (NEAs) are easy to access as they travel around the Sun in very similar orbits to Earth. Additionally, these small bodies have very little mass, and therefore very little gravity, making it easy to extract resources.*

> *Asteroid mining begins with prospecting for the best resources. Then materials are harvested and processed into refined, usable supplies. Finally, these resources can be manufactured into finished products. DSI and its partners are developing end-to-end*

technologies to accomplish these steps in the unique environment of space.

While it might sound crazy to mine asteroids at first, it actually makes a lot of sense when it comes to building things in space. The company explains:

> *Manufacturing in microgravity and hard vacuum offers both opportunities and challenges. The upside of making things in space includes the ability to create very large structures that would never fit into the confines of a launch vehicle's payload fairing. Huge solar arrays to produce energy and enormous antenna to enhance communications satellites are among the possibilities.* [4]

It's incredibly exciting to think that these things, which once seemed so far out of reach and beyond the realm of possibility, are now becoming businesses, with actual funding and research. Once we figure out how to mine asteroids and travel without abiding by the laws of physics -- we might be able to spread humanity as Kardashev envisioned.

When it comes to spreading humanity, though, is this necessarily a good thing? When we're operating in space, it's incredibly important to consider the ethical implications of our own actions – as they may impact the potential evolution of entire civilizations.

If you've seen movies like *Independence Day, War of the Worlds*, or any one of the many Hollywood portrayals of alien encounters, you'll have an idea of what I'm talking about. The plot line is similar in all of them: very sophisticated, powerful aliens come and threaten to destroy life as we know it — be it through war, disease, or just utter disregard for human existence. Usually in

---

4 "Asteroid Mining | Deep Space Industries". 2018. *Deep Space Industries.* http://deepspaceindustries.com/mining/.

these movies, the humans fight back, barely defeating the aliens and destroying most of Earth in the process but living to continue humanity.

We all know how terrifying this thought is, but when going to other planets we have to consider that we may be the ones wreaking havoc on microbial ecosystems (or, potentially, on advanced beings, as well). In any event, alien contact doesn't necessarily have to be here on Earth in order to be bad – it can be just as bad somewhere else.

"If there is life on Mars, I believe we should do nothing with Mars. Mars then belongs to the Martians, even if the Martians are only microbes."— Carl Sagan

There have been many debates about the ethics of finding life on other planets. Some scientists, like the late Carl Sagan, believe that if any life is found on a planet, we should leave it be. What Sagan is talking about is something more like the plot of James Cameron's *Avatar,* which we discussed briefly in the Titan chapter, where humans go to a planet in the Alpha Centauri system and murder a bunch of the natives in order to mine their resources. And while the science in these movies may be fictional, the nature of humanity being portrayed may not be. When it comes to colonizing other planets, some may argue that the main reason anyone takes it seriously is for the preservation of humanity -- so why do any of these alien creatures matter?

Human nature is complex, and as a species we tend to abide by a set of morals, some of which include not wiping out entire species of aliens just because we can. What happens if, in the pursuit of preserving our own humanity, we lose sight of what it means to be human?

Man, Ethics gives me a headache.

Yet it is important to consider the possible ramifications of our decisions before we set out. What will the effect of our arrival be for the planet/moon?

In 1983, James Lovelock and Andrew Watson published a paper entitled, "Biological Homeostasis of the Global Environment: the Parable of Daisyworld." In their paper, they explored the results of a computer simulation designed to mimic the events of an Earth-Sun system. The computer simulation, referred to as Daisyworld, was a hypothetical planet orbiting a star whose radiant energy was slowly increasing and decreasing.

In the original paper, Daisyworld was populated with two types of seeds: black daisies and white daisies. The only difference between the daisies was their color, which affected their albedo (the amount of heat energy that they absorbed from sunlight). The planet's white daisies had a high surface albedo, meaning that they reflected light and heat, keeping the area around them cooled. The black daisies, in contrast, had a low surface albedo and absorbed light and heat, warming the area around them.

The simulation began with an empty, cloudless, and cool planet. The planet had no variables, such as rotation, other life forms, geography, or atmospheric conditions. As the sunlight began to warm the planet, black daisies began to populate the surface, soaking in the heat and warming the planet even more. As the black daisies began to populate most of the surface of the planet, the temperature rose and it began to be too hot for black daisies. The warmer temperatures allowed the seeds of the white daisies to sprout, and as they populated more and more of the planet's surface, the planet began to cool. The planet became too cool for the white daisies, and the black daisies began to flourish once more. This began a negative feedback loop, in which each species of daisies muted the effects of the other and began the cycle again.

This experiment was revolutionary, not because people believed that the world would be changed by populations of daisies, but because it showed the ability of an ecosystem to self-correct and maintain its own homeostasis. The experiment was continued with more complex variables and additions of other species (there was even a strain of gray daisy). The results of each variation maintained that both types of daisy were necessary for the planet to maintain *any* population of daisy.

If we were to go to an empty, lifeless planet, would it be for the benefit of both us and the planet to "introduce the daisies" and begin a cycle of life? These are questions I would like to ask you to consider.

Because, what we do need to remember is that, at the end of it all, the Universe isn't *ours*. *We* didn't create it. *We* don't own it. It is our job to learn about it, explore it, and take care of it. And, as we explore, if we find life on Mars, then maybe, just maybe, we should let the Martians have it. If we, as humanity, would be willing to fight for the right to keep our own planet, why should we be the ones to take someone else's planet from them?

The answers may not be easy, or even readily apparent, but it is important to consider the many different sides of these issues as we venture out into the cosmos. And they are answers we may want to have soon, because the technology is rapidly developing, the funding is rapidly materializing, and it may not be long until we *are* capable of colonizing Mars.

And beyond.

CONCLUSION

—

"What is the greatest single factor keeping humanity tied to Earth?"

I asked this question of almost everyone I spoke to in the course of writing this book, and the answer was unanimous: the cost of leaving. The cost to launch something to space is currently somewhere around $20,000 per metric pound of . . . whatever is moving into space, be it rockets or rocks. If we can get the cost of launching a pound to space in the same range as shipping it across the Earth, this will dramatically increase the timeline for colonizing other bodies.

We have the tech available, and minds capable of pioneering solutions to create cheaper launch systems. With money, drive, and the right people, creating a future where humanity is spread across the solar system is 100% attainable. The first step is producing a system where sending people to space is affordable, and to do that we need people who are excited about even the smallest steps needed along the way.

There are many technologies and applications that are theoretical and waiting to be tested in space, but lack the funding to do so. Scientists have to wait years to get their experiments launched, and have to optimize every part to be as compact and as light as possible, so as to keep costs low. Cutting the cost to launch would enable them to use much more of their budget on developing the actual experiment – as well as the follow-up experiments that must inevitably follow.

Back in June of 2017, an alarm on my phone buzzed, waking me from my ever-so-desired sleep (I was taking an 8 AM coding class. *Over the summer.* Sleep was *definitely* more desirable). I rubbed my eyes, stretched, and sat up, scrolling through my Instagram feed. Swiping through various pictures of friends enjoying their summer, I came across a post from NASA: a short video about an eclipse that would be happening in the U.S. in August. I double tapped to 'like' the post, closed my phone and got up to brush my teeth.

As I stared groggily into the mirror, my mind started to kick into gear, reminding me that I still hadn't been able to debug this simple recursive algorithm from the homework set, that I'd left the wash downstairs, and that what I'd just scrolled past was actually pretty cool. I finished brushing my teeth and did a quick internet search for "eclipse 2017" and realized that the eclipse was actually going to cross over all of North America . . . for the first time in *100 years*. I added a note to my calendar, and went on with my day.

Fast forward two months later: the morning of the eclipse. I set up a chair to watch the eclipse on my back porch, and decided to make a homemade eclipse viewer, carefully crafted from high-quality super-scientific materials (a recycled cracker box and a sheet of aluminum foil).

I dug through the recycle and found the perfect vessel, a flattened Kashi box with just the right proportions to make a viewer. I went to the kitchen and taped up the corners of my creation. As I prepared to cut the viewing holes, my 14-year-old brother, Ryan, walked in. When he saw what I was doing, he rolled his eyes, and asked, *"Why are you making that? It's kinda pointless; it's just looking at the sun."*

As I started to explain to him that seeing an eclipse was actually a rare occasion, he poured himself a glass of water and walked out, without even listening to me finish a sentence. *Teenagers . . . I thought to myself. Why aren't they interested in anything other than video games?*

Entertainment has advanced so far since the early days of space exploration, to the point where computer generated content rivals the natural world. For my and future generations, the experiences of a digitally rendered world have become equivalent to, and in some cases surpassed, the beauty of reality. When you can play a game that takes place on a realistic alien planet, an eclipse doesn't sound that cool.

As I completed the finishing touches of my pinhole viewer, I thought back to the first time I watched a rocket land on a drone ship in the ocean. Though it was an incredibly exciting moment from an engineering and scientific viewpoint, from a cinematic standpoint there wasn't much to show: a blurry little line in a cloud of orange smoke stood upright on the screen, and then a room full of engineers clapped.

Even though this was an absolutely awe-inspiring feat for mankind, its spectacle cannot compete with what has become commonplace in movies and television. The astounding nature of this moment would have been lost had I expected a Hollywood quality production with a soundtrack and CGI effects.

I snapped back to reality as my mom called and said she was running late, telling me, *"Ryan has volleyball practice today, could you please drive him? It starts at 2:30."* My heart sank, knowing that the eclipse would happen over my house at 2:48, but I agreed to take him with the hope that there would be a place to watch near the gym.

We got into the car, and he again made fun of my creation. *"That thing is so janky,"* he laughed, calling me a nerd before proceeding to play games on his phone in silence for the rest of the drive (meanwhile, I pondered the meaning of the word *"janky,"* and concluded that it was definitely *not* a compliment).

When we arrived at the gym, Ryan informed me that we were too early, and that his practice started at 3. This meant that we would have to sit outside and wait, but it also meant that I wouldn't miss the eclipse.

As the time neared 2:40, a group of kids from the gym's summer camp came out of the building, and their counselor handed out eclipse glasses. As the clouds parted for a moment, one of the little girls shouted in excitement that she could see the moon. All the other kids began staring up at the sun, and I turned around to watch the shadow in my box. I felt a tug on my shirt and looked down to see the same little girl who had been shouting staring up at me with awe in her eyes.

"You made your own glasses?" she asked. *"Why do you have to stand the other way?"*

I explained that my creation was a pinhole viewer, which shows the shadow of the eclipse rather than directly viewing it. She offered to trade me for her glasses, so I handed her my box and expected her to want a trade back immediately, but as she turned her back and held it up, she grinned.

I put on the glasses and looked directly at the eclipse. Seeing the tiny orange sliver of the sun immediately moved me, and I felt tears welling up in my eyes. I called Ryan over, and told him he had to take a look. His interest was piqued, as the kids around us had all become silent, which is quite rare for the group of energetic 6 year olds. He spent a few seconds looking up through the glasses, and then asked the girl to trade back for my box. As the time ticked past 2:48 we had reached the peak of the eclipse that we could see,

81% coverage, and the kids began to chatter again, every one of them gushing about their views. Ryan turned to me, and *actually admitted* that he had been wrong about the eclipse being lame, but was quick to defend himself that my box was *"way less cool"* than the glasses we had borrowed.

There is nothing quite like witnessing an event in person. In the case of the eclipse, we'd all seen photos and renderings of an eclipse before, but something about that orange sliver and the shadow on the box was enough to bring tears to my eyes, as well as pacify a group of rambunctious 6 year olds into silence. Even Ryan, who had been certain that it was a waste of time and effort (and is well-known to be the most stubborn child in the family), admitted that seeing the eclipse was one of the most exciting things he'd done all summer.

Thinking back to that morning when I had seen NASA's Instagram post, I now wonder how we can make studying space more exciting for everyone. Because, leading up to the eclipse, I noticed that there were tons of ads for eclipse glasses, lots of advice on how to be safe when watching the eclipse, instructions on where to see it in totality, stats on past eclipses, and other info about the event. I was pleasantly surprised to find that so many folks had taken an interest in science, space, and nature. What stuck out to me though, was the lack of staying power. Once the social media trend was over, space stopped being cool again. Yes, getting people excited on social media is a start, but something *more* needs to happen.

With the advancement of CGI and incredible science fiction media, real science must up its game as well. Most kids aren't interested in reading a technical paper, but they love seeing science in action. Science doesn't have to be dry, and it doesn't have to be fiction to be exciting, either. So how are companies like SpaceX engaging audiences that normally wouldn't care?

By making it a spectacle.

Elon Musk is well known for his fun, clever, and unconventional naming schemes. Musk's most recent venture into the market of drilling underground tunnels is aptly named The Boring Company. His electric car company is named after Nikola Tesla, the scientist credited for inventing the alternating current electric induction motor. Tesla now produces 3 models of cars: Tesla's 4 door luxury sedan is known as the Model S, the SUV Model X, and most recently the smaller and more affordable Model 3 sedan. Originally, Tesla filed for the name Model E for their most recent car, but was blocked by a patent from Ford. Maybe you can guess where this is headed. The decision to go with Model 3 gives Tesla a product line of Model S, 3, X. How clever.

The naming schemes at SpaceX have also followed the trend, with the Falcon series of rockets named after Han Solo's famous smuggling freighter, *Millennium Falcon*. The Dragon Capsule, SpaceX's passenger spacecraft, was named after the 1963 song, "Puff, the Magic Dragon," by Peter, Paul and Mary, as a response to critics who claimed that his projects were impossible. And, of course, as we saw in Chapter 2, the newest series of SpaceX rockets is called the BFR.

Along with his affinity for unique and inspiring names, Musk is also known to put on a spectacle. From hiding Easter eggs, such as "*Santa Mode,*" in Tesla vehicles, to selling branded "Temperature Enhancement Devices" (Flamethrowers) to raise money for The Boring Company, he's always game to put on a show. The latest Musk-related spectacle is the launch of SpaceX's Falcon Heavy rocket, which carried Musk's own cherry-red Tesla Roadster to orbit Mars.

"Test flights of new rockets usually contain mass simulators in the form of concrete or steel blocks. That seemed extremely boring. Of course, anything boring is terrible, especially companies, so we decided to send something unusual, something that made us

feel. The payload will be an original Tesla Roadster, playing Space Oddity, on a billion year elliptic Mars orbit." -Elon Musk

Elon Musk is creating spectacles that grab the public's attention and inspire people to take an interest in space. I hope this book does something similar, and has helped you to better understand what's going on, why we're doing it, and where it might lead us. I realize that even as I am here, writing this book for you, some of the information is going out of date. Every day, something new is discovered, inventions are made, test results are analyzed, and papers are published. While I've tried to include the most up-to-date information possible, things change, sometimes rapidly. The best way to keep informed is to keep asking questions, supporting science, and keep spreading the word when you hear about something exciting.

I hope that reading this book has given you insight into the technologies being developed that will help us answer the question of where in the solar system, after Mars, humans will inhabit next. Hopefully, and most importantly, it has given you the chance to form your own opinions about our future in space.

Arthur C. Clarke once wrote that new ideas pass through three periods:

- "It can't be done."
- "It probably can be done, but it's not worth doing."
- "I knew it was a good idea all along!"

If you are to take away one thing from reading this, it should be that colonizing space is not only possible, but that it is worth doing. One day, perhaps sooner than we think, we will be able to look out at the stars, board our ships, and boldly go where no one has gone before.

www.ingramcontent.com/pod-product-compliance
Lightning Source LLC
Chambersburg PA
CBHW071524180526
45171CB00002B/369